Contents

1 Introducing addiction

And Noah the husbandman began, and planted a vineyard.
And he drank of the wine, and was drunken; and he was
uncovered within his tent.

Genesis IX

The use of mind-altering drugs is as old as mankind. Fermented beverages were probably used by prehistoric man, and the uses of wine and beer are described in the earliest writings of ancient Egypt. Opium and marijuana have been used for centuries, and the stimulant properties of the coca plant were known to the Indians of South America centuries before the Spanish conquest.

The Bible mentions wine more than 165 times in generally approving terms, but it warns strongly against drunkenness. Even in Biblical times, the essential problem is posed: How can we enjoy the benefits of drugs without risking the problems that can so easily accompany their use?

The search for a perspective

Even in ancient times it was known that the use of a drug, whether as a medicine or for recreation, sometimes produced unwanted effects. The history of using drugs to excess or in a manner frowned upon by society ('drug abuse', as we would now call it) is as long as mankind's. Hogarth's marvellously horrifying engravings give us some idea of the problems caused by 'penny gin' in England 300 years ago, and make our own 'drug culture' seem somewhat less frightful—and less new. Intoxication with alcohol can lead to accidents, embarrassing losses of social inhibition, or violence. Too big a dose of an opiate, whether for pain or pleasure, may cause death. Hallucinogens may lead you to believe you can fly unaided: with fatal consequences if you try to do so.

Inevitably, each society develops rules and guidelines for the use of drugs—defining the uses and behaviours that are acceptable and others that are moderately disapproved of; which drugs may be self-administered, which are taken only on the advice of a

*'Six children and a
habit to support,
please, mister...'*

priest or medicine-man; and the drugs that are absolutely forbidden. What is acceptable for one individual may be forbidden to another. In some countries, for example, men may drink to intoxication, but women and children who do the same are criticised, viewed as deviant and may be punished.

The acceptability of drugs varies greatly from culture to culture. Even within a culture it may change greatly as time passes. Alcohol, so widely accepted in Western society, is roundly condemned and prohibited in Moslem cultures where marijuana is often tolerated. Opium, once a widely accepted recreational drug in the East and available in grocery stores until the late 19th century in England and the United States, is now prohibited (except when used as a medicine). Tobacco, once severely condemned, is now universally permitted, although in recent times its use is becoming less acceptable. The use of such psychedelics ('mind-manifesting' drugs) as LSD, mescalin and psilocybin, so recently viewed in Western countries as a matter of intellectual curiosity and personal choice for a few, was soon redefined as an 'abuse' and outlawed when their use spread to larger numbers during the 'psychedelic revolution' of the 1960s. In the United States, the use of cocaine is now illegal; 75 years ago it was an ingredient that helped make Coca Cola 'the pause that refreshes'.[1]

In public... or behind closed doors—but the urge is the same, and the need as dire.

Uses and abuses

The social and economic problems a drug causes do not always correlate with a society's attitudes towards it. Alcohol has brought in its wake incalculable human misery. Nevertheless, its long traditions of use and its social acceptability in Western culture make it unlikely that any serious attempt will be made to outlaw it or even to reduce its availability. Where such restriction has been attempted—wholly, as in Prohibition in the United States, or partly, as in some Scandinavian countries—much human ingenuity has gone into frustrating the attempt. Tobacco, now recognised by all nations of the world as a causal factor in many serious illnesses, is rarely regarded as a 'drug of abuse' and in many developing nations—and among women in developed ones—its use is increasing.

Dependence and addiction

With certain drugs, repeated use may lead to a change in the way the user and the drug interact. The capacity of the user to choose where and when to use the drug is gradually reduced. There is a loss of plasticity or autonomy. In extreme cases, the user seems to be completely unable to control drug use—to be overwhelmingly involved with the use of the drug and with securing its supply—even when this means a reordering of his or her usual values. There is also a high tendency to resume drug use after a period of abstinence.

For several hundred years scholars and laymen have been debating about the causes of this loss of plasticity—and about what to call it. When tobacco was first introduced into England, those who seemed unable or unwilling to give up smoking were likened to 'drunkards', a concept which has been around since biblical times. In the early 1700s the behaviour was viewed in moral terms—the drinker deviated from his society's norms concerning alcohol as a result of his 'lack of will' and for 'love of wine'.[2] Similar moral views were held about those who were unable to stop using opium.

Then in 1700, the English physician, John Jones, wrote:

> The effects of sudden leaving off the uses of opium after a long and lavish use thereof [were] great and intolerable distresses, anxieties and depressions of spirit, which commonly end in a most miserable death, attended with strange agonies, unless men return to the use of opium; which soon raises them again, and certainly restores them.

He attributed these 'effects of sudden leaving off', this *withdrawal syndrome*, to toxic impurities in the opium, and the difficulty that some people have in giving up opium to their inability to tolerate the misery of withdrawal. This was the beginning of the disease concept as an alternative to the moralistic view that drug users simply lacked willpower. The tremulousness and delirium that occur with heavy alcohol use were first described at the turn of the 19th century, but at the time these symptoms were not immediately recognised as caused by cessation of alcohol use.

By the end of the 18th century a number of divergent views about the causes of this 'need' or 'desire' to use a drug, this loss of plasticity, had emerged. It was seen as immorality—an indifference to what God and man viewed as proper, or as a defect of willpower, or as a special love for the effects of the drug, which developed only in certain vulnerable individuals or groups. With opiates, the lower classes were viewed as more vulnerable to developing such a 'love' than the upper or middle classes. Others argued that the need or desire was a physical disorder brought about by the actions of a drug on the body. Yet another view was that the condition might simply be a strong habit that develops, like other habits, after many repetitions.[2]

Naming the need

The names attached to this need or desire for drugs varied with the times and the perspective of the observer. The word 'addiction' (from the Latin, meaning given over to a master, enslaved) was applied early to drug-using behaviours, including smoking. Interestingly, the term was also applied (perhaps even earlier) to a number of behaviours which were unrelated to drug use but also involved a loss of plasticity. People who seemed inordinately involved with gambling or card playing were also described as being 'addicted'.

When the use of alcohol was the major problem, words like 'inebriate' and 'drunkard' were common. The word 'inebriate'

An 'addiction' or just
a pastime? The
borderline can be hard
to define.

was later applied to those who used opiates—along with terms
like 'habitué'.

Why such concern about words and terminology? At the
centre of much of the difficulty that surrounds the topic of drug
use, misuse, dependence and addiction is the difficulty of
agreeing on a definition of the problem. Without definitions, the
epidemiologist cannot count cases to see how the incidence and
prevalence of a disease varies from place to place or from time to
time or is affected by social and economic conditions. Without
definitions, the clinician cannot summarise his findings on which
individuals improve with a particular treatment; and without
definitions that separate a 'case' from a 'non-case', researchers
cannot study the biology or the psychology of a syndrome and
cannot tell us about causes and consequences.

Despite the importance of the matter, experts still find it
difficult to agree. There was so much confusion about the
meaning of the terms 'addiction' and 'habituation' that an
Expert Committee of the World Health Organisation abandoned
these terms in 1965 and adopted the more neutral term 'drug
dependence'. The committee defined drug dependence as:

A state, psychic and sometimes also physical, resulting from
the interaction between a living organism and a drug,
characterised by behavioural and other responses that always
include a compulsion to take the drug on a continuous or
periodic basis in order to experience its psychic effects, and
sometimes to avoid the discomfort of its absence. Tolerance
may or may not be present. A person may be dependent on
more than one drug.

The committee was more comfortable with pharmacology than psychiatry, psychology or sociology and attempted to categorise patterns of drug dependence in terms of the drug involved. They recognised the impossibility of describing each drug individually and tried to group drugs together into categories in which the effects of the drugs and the behavioural patterns seen when dependence develops appeared similar. The committee proposed nine categories or classes of dependence-producing substances: the alcohol-barbiturate group; amphetamine-like substances; cannabis (marijuana, hashish); cocaine; hallucinogens (LSD and related drugs); *khat* (a stimulant used in Yemen and Ethiopia); opiates (opioids: the term opiate is generally used to refer to drugs made from opium directly or indirectly that have morphine-like effects; opioid is a broader term including both opiates and a wide variety of totally synthetic substances which have morphine-like effects); volatile solvents and tobacco.[3] The characteristics of these groups will be discussed individually in other chapters.

Although such a classification by drug groups is valuable, drug users do not often fit neatly into the categories. Many users employ different drugs depending on such factors as availability, cost, desired interactive effects of multiple drugs, likelihood of detection of their use of a particular drug, or their momentary inclination. Many who begin with one substance go on to use others. 'Polydrug abuse'—the use of multiple drugs—is common, as are its complications.

The present terminology poses an even greater difficulty for which there is still no easy solution. This is the extraordinary diversity of behaviours and people that can be included under a

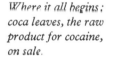

Where it all begins: coca leaves, the raw product for cocaine, on sale.

single designation such as 'drug dependence morphine type'. This can range from the repeatedly described antisocial urban 'junkie' (heroin addict) found in large Western cities to the medical practitioner whose first use of, say, the synthetic opioid meperidine for severe headaches has become a dependence and interferes with his generally satisfactory work. There are also the hill tribesmen of Laos and Thailand who smoke opium and experience only moderate difficulties with work and social adjustment.

The patterns of drug use and social adjustment that can be included under each of the other drug types are no less diverse. Furthermore, the WHO was not entirely successful in persuading the world to give up terms like 'alcoholism' and 'addiction'. If the term 'addiction' is used here, at all, it will be used to convey the notion of an extreme on a continuum of involvement with the use of a drug; an involvement that takes over other values in the user's life.

Since there is no sharp line which separates a heavy drug user from someone who is 'dependent', even experts have some difficulty in agreeing on definitions in any given case—unless the behaviour is extreme. Some writers use terms like 'compulsive drug use' to describe the pattern seen in dependence;[4] others have argued that some forms of dependence would hardly merit so strong a term. Recently, groups of experts have been meeting to agree on criteria so that when they conduct research, one 'expert' will know just what problem another 'expert' is looking at—but there are still no universally accepted definitions.[2]

What does dependence mean?

It was formerly believed that only a drug which causes 'physical dependence'—that is, produces biological changes so that withdrawal symptoms appear when the drug is discontinued—could produce a severe dependence syndrome. Drugs which did not produce such changes merely caused 'habituation' or 'psychological dependence'. This distinction, although beguiling in its simplicity, is misleading. Stopping the use of tobacco or amphetamine does not produce withdrawal symptoms that are as visible and predictable as does heroin, yet both can be associated with behavioural patterns that are exceedingly difficult to modify. Millions of smokers throughout the world can attest to the difficulties of giving cigarettes up once hooked; and even heroin addicts have frequently commented that giving up smoking was more difficult than stopping their heroin use. Heavy amphetamine users often find the compulsion to continue use overwhelming—despite the havoc this use is creating in their lives. In fact, withdrawal syndromes do follow the discontinuation of tobacco or amphetamine, but the relationship between a withdrawal syndrome and drug dependence is extremely complex.[4]

There are a number of drugs which, if given repeatedly over a long period, produce *physical dependence* and therefore a *withdrawal syndrome* when they are discontinued. But for many of these drugs the syndrome is not necessarily accompanied by severe discomfort, anxiety or a marked desire to get more of the drug. So physical dependence need not equal 'addiction' or 'psychological dependence'. A good example of this is the drug imipramine, which is used in the treatment of depression; when it is stopped after prolonged administration, there may be nausea, muscle aches, anxiety and difficulty in sleeping but never a compulsion to resume the use of the drug.[4]

The beginnings of dependence

Recent studies show that for the opioid drugs, and probably for alcohol and barbiturates as well, the biological changes that lead to physical dependence begin with the first dose.[4] For example, if a patient is given an opioid several times a day to relieve pain following surgery, it would be possible by using an 'opioid antagonist' to show that the patient had developed a modest degree of physical dependence of the opioid type by the second or third day. Yet patients are treated with opioids in this way hundreds of thousands of times each year and virtually none becomes psychologically dependent or addicted. Most drug experts would probably agree that it is psychological dependence more than any other single factor which lies at the heart of what the average person thinks of when he hears the term drug addiction.

Why is it, then, that some people will seek out a drug, even if it is prohibited in their society, and eventually come to feel that they cannot get along without it, while others seem to be able to stop its use with only slight difficulty even when physical dependence is induced? How much is due to the drug, how much to the individual and how much to the circumstances in which the interaction takes place?

Despite many years of research, the answers to these questions are still in doubt. But partial explanations abound, and, just as important, we think we are learning to ask better questions. We now recognise that there are distinct stages in the natural history of drug use and dependence and that different factors can have their impact at different stages. Researchers now ask which factors (psychological, sociological, biological, pharmacological) determine whether there will be *initial use* (*experimentation*), whether an initial user will repeat the experience and become a *casual* or *recreational* user, whether such a user will go on to heavy or *intensive use*, or to dependence (*compulsive use*, *addiction* and in the case of alcohol, *alcoholism*). We need also to ask the same questions about what leads to *relapse* after a period of abstinence.

It may be that we have simply coined new terms to express the same ideas that were debated in the 19th century, but most of those working on the problem feel that some progress has been made along the way.

11

2 Why are drugs abused?

'Spiritual' explanations for the universal interest in mind-altering drugs abound in the histories of every society. These explanations may be no worse than others based on a scientific proposition. There are new theories about the presence of endogenous opioid-like substances in the brain, but as far as we know the capacity to experience pleasure from drug use has no survival value.

Yet some mechanism is clearly at work to promote the interaction between human beings and drugs. Animals are susceptible as well. In one of Ian Fleming's books[1] a fastidious villain asks James Bond, a smoker of tobacco, whether he could envisage 'a cow taking lighted straw into its mouth and inhaling the smoke'. In fact, animals can be taught to smoke tobacco, albeit with great difficulty. Animals will take almost any drug a man will take, and with much the same enthusiasm. If they are allowed free access to a drug, there will be similar side effects and behavioural consequences.

Drugs as reinforcers

Laboratory animals such as monkeys and rats with catheters implanted in a vein will learn to press a lever to self-administer opioid drugs, barbiturates or alcohol, and they will do so even when the periods of self-administration are spaced so as to prevent the development of physical dependence. They will press many times for a single injection. If the drugs are not too bitter, animals will also learn to drink or eat them.[1]

In this sense, certain drugs are powerful reinforcers of drug-using behaviour: their acute effects increase the likelihood that the behaviour will occur again. Not all drugs are reinforcers. Some drugs are punishers: they decrease the likelihood that an animal will engage in drug self-administration. For example, animals will avoid administering the tranquilliser chlorpromazine. But in general they will self-administer most of the same drugs taken by man: opioids, amphetamines, cocaine, alcohol and barbiturates.

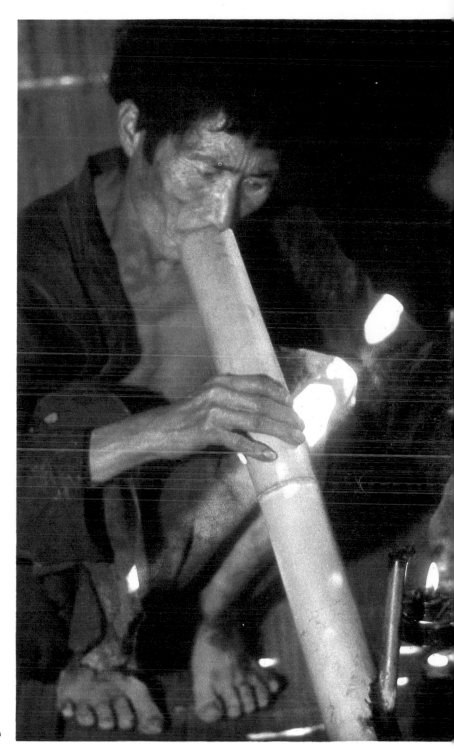

Some can try a drug once and never take it again... others grow old with their habit. Why these differences?

13

Who said that breaking the habit isn't easy.

LSD is one drug which is not self-administered. Neither is cannabis, unless the animal has first learned to self-administer PCP, another mind-altering drug. Animals will inject nicotine but compared to cocaine it is a weak reinforcer indeed. Caffeine is a modest reinforcer.[1]

We still do not know why some drugs are reinforcers while others are not. The reinforcers do not share any single action on the brain and they clearly produce very different subjective mental states. People and laboratory animals can readily categorise drugs that are reinforcers into eight or nine distinct groups. The morphine-like opioids are recognised as similar and are easily distinguished from other classes, despite chemical differences. Cannabis (marijuana) appears to represent a distinct class which is different from LSD and both are distinct from PCP. Nicotine, too, is in a class of its own.

Recent research suggests that several distinct brain systems each with its own chemistry may underlie the reinforcing effects of different drugs.[1] Even more fascinating is the observation that what is a reinforcer depends on the history of the animal and environmental conditions. Under certain circumstances, animals will continue to press a lever to get an unpleasant electrical current of the same intensity that they previously worked hard to avoid.[2]

Why don't we all use drugs?

If so many drugs are inherently reinforcing, why doesn't everyone use them almost continuously? Unlike laboratory animals, humans have access to many other positive reinforcers. These include sex, the rewards of interpersonal relationships and tasty foods. Continuous drug use might be incompatible with these rewards.

An equally powerful reason is that every society has found it necessary to structure and place limits on the use of drugs. Where such structuring has not occurred—as with tobacco use in many cultures—use is almost universal and continuous. It is limited only by the adverse effects of high doses and by the cost and availability of the drug.

Social attitudes to the use of a drug, its cost and general availability determine who will experiment with it. Tobacco and alcohol experimentation or use are almost universal in Western society; experimentation with marijuana is common but experience with heroin is not. Having easy access to drugs may be a factor in dependency: doctors and nurses have much higher rates of addiction than other occupational groups.

But even availability and habitual use do not inevitably result in persistent use and repeated relapse. During the Vietnamese war, thousands of American soldiers used pure heroin for many months. Almost 50 per cent of the regular users became physically dependent. Despite this, when they returned home most (over 90 per cent) were able to discontinue this use unaided, primarily because the drug was no longer cheaply available and the social attitudes towards its use were more negative.[3]

Peer group influence

Drug use by friends and acquaintances has been found to be an important determinant of a person's drug experience. For example, some ethnic and national groups make far more extensive use of alcohol than do others. During one's teens, the need to conform to what others in the same age group are doing is often strong. This applies to drug-taking—or *not* drug-taking—as much as to wearing jeans or a particular hairstyle.

When a drug such as LSD or marijuana is not legally available beginner users are supplied by their friends, from whom they have learnt to use it. This is why illicit drug use has been described as a kind of communicable disease which spreads from user to user. Although we should not carry such analogies too far, we ought to note that even the use of legal drugs like tobacco and alcohol are initially communicated from one young person to another. One neighbour may recommend to another a particularly useful drug for 'nerves' that had been prescribed by the local doctor.

Who is vulnerable?

Peer pressure and the boredom of an isolated existence—military services overseas, for example—seem to encourage experimentation with and continued use of a drug as an escape from tedium.

But even when drug abuse is very common, there are those who resist regular use and do not continue to the point of dependence. This is obvious to anyone familiar with alcohol use. Surprising as it may seem, only a small percentage of those who experiment with the opioids, including heroin, become regular users. During the peak of the American drug epidemic of the late 1960s national surveys revealed that approximately six per cent of young men had tried heroin at least once in their lives, but only a tiny fraction admitted to current use within the preceding 30 days.[3]

In the 1930s, the psychoanalyst Rado expressed the view that a pre-existing 'tense depression' sensitises the future addict to the drug-induced pleasurable effects, and that the euphoria of the drug effect is quickly followed by a return to the state of depression which is even less tolerable than it was before the drug use. Rado also observed that the addict was intolerant to pain and was receptive to the euphoric effects of a variety of drugs which transformed him into a more optimistic and self-confident individual.

In some ways, Rado's formulation anticipates the recent findings of William Martin and his colleagues at the Addiction Research Center in Lexington, Kentucky. These researchers noted that opioid addicts who were prisoners seemed to be tense, depressed, dysphoric and intolerant of pain. They experienced increased self-esteem and confidence not only when they used opioids, but also after taking high doses of various other substances, such as amphetamines, alcohol and barbiturates.

Isidor Chein and his colleagues described young heroin addicts

15

Tribal unity in a cloud of smoke—or a lonely retreat behind a smokescreen.

in New York as having a profound sense of inadequacy and low self-esteem coupled with an inability to find everyday satisfaction in work and in their relations with others. Heroin provided a powerfully pleasurable tension reduction that temporarily annihilated other needs.

Alcoholics have been described as depressed, hostile people with difficulty in feeling close to others, who typically relate to them in immature and dependent ways. Some researchers emphasise psychopathy as the common denominator: 'addicts' in this view are immature, demanding 'instant gratification' of their needs, lacking in moral compunction and exploitative of other people.[4]

The nonconformists

Such descriptions are all very well in their way, but there are many who conform to them who do *not* become drug dependent. In the same way many do *not* match these stereotypes but become seriously dependent on drugs. It seems likely that many experimental users 'like' the effects of opioids, amphetamines and other drugs (some more than others) but most are also concerned about avoiding the bad effects (social and medical) that come with continued use. However, those who are depressed and who see little likelihood that life will be better in the future will have lost the major incentive that motivates others to stop experimenting.

In the past, it was assumed that the decreased self-esteem and depression that is so common in drug users was due exclusively to unhappy early family experiences or current economic, social and familiar stresses. It may be, however, that the increased sense of wellbeing that some users experience can also be a result of biological factors.

Several researchers have postulated that some biochemical abnormality might make some people experience either euphoria or a 'normalising' effect when they first use opioids. Recent reseach indicates that there may be a genetic factor that makes some people vulnerable to alcoholism.[5] As yet, there is no information showing a genetic vulnerability to opioid or barbiturate use, but the possibility that addiction involves some subtle 'deficiency disease' or dysregulation of the brain's function is now getting a lot of attention.

Drs Vincent Dole and Marie Nyswander, who pioneered the use of methadone—a synthetic narcotic—in the long-term maintenance treatment of heroin addicts, were early advocates of this view. Heroin addiction, they reasoned, is a deficiency disease roughly analogous to diabetes, in which a substance normally present in and needed by the body is lacking. When this need is met by daily doses either of heroin or its substitute, methadone, the addict is able to function normally.

Withdrawal and tolerance

The way people respond to the symptoms that result from discontinuing a drug—withdrawal—varies, as does the severity of the symptoms from case to case. For some drugs (alcohol, barbiturates) withdrawal of heavy dosage can be life-endangering; for others, such as opioids, withdrawal may be painful and extremely distressing, if relatively safe. Fear of such consequences can be an important factor in maintaining drug dependence.

Tolerance means that with repeated use of a drug the user requires increasingly larger amounts to produce the effects originally experienced. He may eventually be using quantities many times those which a non-user could take without injury. But tolerance does not develop uniformly to all aspects of a drug's effects. Users of alcohol and barbiturates become tolerant to the *intoxication* action, but the potentially *lethal* dose does not change appreciably. So the amount the user feels the need of may be nearly enough to kill.[6]

Calming the nerves

Users of opioids or alcohol often say that they take these drugs to relieve anxiety (calm their nerves) or to make them feel better in various ways. They may produce a 'high' or relieve depression. Such effects do occur in some cases when drug use begins. But this is not what is seen when alcoholics or opioid users are allowed to use their drugs continuously for several weeks in a laboratory situation. In both alcoholics and opioid addicts, tolerance develops to the euphoria and antidepressant effects. After the first week of use, there is increased anxiety, irritability and depressed mood.[7, 8] Yet both groups continue. Why?

The avoidance of withdrawal does not fully account for persistent use. Alcoholics will often let themselves go into withdrawal by deciding to stop abruptly. Opioid users, on the other hand, do not usually let themselves go into withdrawal without some external pressure. However, unlike alcoholics, they continue to experience brief episodes of euphoria following each drug injection—even though their overall mood is one of depression and irritability.[8] Nevertheless, withdrawal symptoms do play an important role in the development of psychological dependence and in relapse as described in the next section. And while the dramatic, distressing and life-threatening withdrawal symptoms have largely run their course after a week or two, subtle disturbances of physiology may persist for weeks or months, making former users more vulnerable to stress.

Learning to use drugs

For any kind of behaviour, the more rapidly the reward follows the behaviour and the more often the behaviour is rewarded, the stronger the 'learning' or habit becomes. Drug use is no exception to this rule.

For example, if a drug is used intravenously or by inhalation so that the reinforcing effects occur immediately, a strong habit can quickly develop. If the drug is short-acting so that it must be taken many times a day (as with nicotine, alcohol or cocaine) there are many opportunities for 'reinforcing' the drug-using behaviour. If, in addition, the drug is one that causes physical dependence and the withdrawal syndrome is distressing (aversive), a new condition or mechanism of reinforcement comes into being. Each time the drug is stopped, there is distress that is relieved by taking the drug. And again, if the drug is short-acting and must be taken many times a day to avoid withdrawal, there are many opportunities for reinforcing drug behaviour.

So drugs that are reinforcers and also cause physical dependence create two mechanisms that lead to highly reinforced behaviour—the primary drug effect and relief of withdrawal distress. Complete tolerance may not develop to the primary reinforcing effects of drugs like opioids or nicotine even after months of use. Both mechanisms may thus operate at the same time to increase the strength of the learned behaviour.

Who can be taught—and how?

Where social use of a drug is viewed as highly deviant and the drug is obtained illegally, most experimenters begin with some personality problems. But the learning process described can, theoretically, be superimposed on relatively 'normal' personalities, and neither psychopathology nor adverse socio-economic conditions are necessary to account for dependence and relapse after withdrawal. The possibility of dependence without personality disturbance can be easily seen with drugs like nicotine, but it can also occur when patients take opioids, sleeping pills or tranquillisers on the advice of their doctors.

There are other ways that learning contributes to dependence and relapse. Dr Abraham Wikler proposed that the withdrawal syndrome can be viewed as unconditioned response—a response to the removal of the drug from its receptors. The salivation in

Mainlining—fast train to the terminal.

*The end of the road...
or perhaps the first
step to rehabilitation.*

Pavlov's dogs was an unconditioned response which was originally elicited by the taste of meat. This became 'conditioned' to the sound of a bell. In the same way, the withdrawal syndrome can become linked or 'conditioned' to the environmental conditions (stimuli) under which withdrawal occurs. This conditioned withdrawal has been seen in animals and humans in the case of opioids and alcohol. It is probably a general principle that applies to other drugs that produce physical dependence and withdrawal.

Once this conditioning or associative learning occurs, elements of the withdrawal syndrome, with its sense of 'craving' for more drugs, can be elicited by environmental stimuli long after the individual has been withdrawn from opioid drugs.

Thus the opioid addict, who feels no craving while in a hospital or a therapeutic community, may feel a need for a 'fix' when he returns to his home environment where he used drugs and experienced withdrawal. Dr Charles O'Brien and his colleagues at the University of Pennsylvania, have shown that opioid effects and opioid withdrawal can be linked or conditioned in human opiate addicts to the smell of peppermint oil. Among O'Brien's subjects the most powerful stimulus for eliciting craving was being offered some 'dope' by a friend.[9] Under the usual circumstances, the addict does not distinguish between 'real withdrawal' and 'conditioned withdrawal'. Both states are experienced as intense craving and both are relieved by the injection of an opioid drug.

Craving a fix

Unfortunately, in the process of alleviating conditioned withdrawal or 'craving', the addict who may have spent weeks withdrawing from the drug (whether it was an opioid, alcohol or tobacco) reinitiates the entire vicious cycle. According to Wikler, even emotions can act as conditioned stimuli. Thus, if anger or anxiety become linked with withdrawal, these feelings can later elicit a withdrawal syndrome and its accompanying 'craving' for the drug. After a while, the addict begins to interpret all unpleasant emotions as 'craving' and responds to all such feelings with the use of a drug.

This explanation of 'craving' as conditioned withdrawal has also been used to account for the craving experienced by alcoholics and smokers when they see someone else 'light up', or even when they drink that cup of coffee that formerly accompanied a cigarette.

Dependence and relapse seem to involve a number of factors. These include individual vulnerability (which in turn may involve personality, environmental and biological factors), social attitudes, and the availability of the specific drug as well as learning and conditioning. One factor may predominate in a given case, but it is likely that all of these factors play some role in every case of dependence across a wide spectrum of drugs.

3 Pursuing the poppy

During the major part of the 19th century, opiates, in the form of patent medicines, were widely used in Europe, England and the United States. These medicines were given to children to quiet them, taken by ladies who felt embarrassed to drink alcohol, and used by alcoholics who were trying to give up strong liquor. Although the opiate withdrawal syndrome had been described as early as 1700, this did not seem to discourage physicians from prescribing opiates or the general public from using them.

Opium and the pure drug morphine (which had been isolated from opium in 1803) were used regularly by a remarkably diverse group of people. Many were upright and productive citizens, with no apparent problems; some were individuals who formerly had alcohol problems.[1] In the cities, opiates were also used by criminals, gamblers and prostitutes. They were generally taken by mouth, but some users were already beginning to inject them by means of the newly introduced hypodermic needle.

Growing concern

Meanwhile, social concern about opiate use was growing progressively more intense on both sides of the Atlantic. In the United States, some experts saw much of the problem of opiate dependence as due to over-prescribing by physicians. Others blamed the use of opiates in patent medicine. It was generally felt that there was a need to restrict opiates to situations where they were medically necessary and make them available only on a doctor's prescription.

It was not until the beginning of this century that these restrictions on opiate drugs took effect in England and the United States. The limited availability of the opiates was made more tolerable by the introduction of a new painkilling drug, aspirin, and a new class of drugs for anxiety—the barbiturates.

Flower-power—
the opium poppy.

21

Meet the opiate family

Morphine is the pure drug that gives opium its characteristic actions. Because it was found to be as likely as opium to cause dependence, chemists began to look for a way to change the morphine molecule in the hope that they could separate the beneficial effects from the toxic and unwanted effects. Among morphine's useful effects are the relief of pain, suppression of cough, reduction of movements of the intestine (making morphine an excellent drug for the treatment of diarrhoea) and the induction of a state of indifference to threatening situations. The unwanted effects include nausea and vomiting, the development of tolerance and physical dependence, and depression of breathing. Some experts felt that the sense of unusual wellbeing (euphoria) that morphine produced was a useful effect for the sick and distressed; others believed that this euphoria was undesirable and led to dependence.

A large number of morphine derivatives were made, but most of them had similar effects to the parent drug. An early derivative was made by treating morphine with acetic anhydride to yield diacetyl morphine. In 1898, it was introduced into medicine as a cough suppressant under the name 'heroin'. Heroin was indeed a good cough suppressant and produced fewer side effects than morphine. But within 20 years it had acquired a bad reputation in the United States, because of its popularity among addicts in urban areas. Its production in the United States was prohibited, but it continues to be used as a useful therapeutic agent in England even today.

'Will it hurt for long, Doctor?'

Pethidine and methadone

Just before the Second World War, German chemists discovered two new series of molecules which were chemically unrelated to morphine, yet seemed to produce similar effects. Meperidine, or pethidine, was the first member of one series and was introduced into medicine under the trade name Demerol. It is still in use today. Methadone, the first member of the other family, was introduced into medicine as Dolophine or Physeptone. It, too, is still in use.

By the mid-1940s, many derivatives of these synthetic analgesics as well as of the natural opiate morphine had been tried and found to be similar to morphine in both good and bad effects. The term *opioid* was coined to refer collectively to natural opiates (derived directly or indirectly from opium) and the newer, totally synthetic substances with identical effects to those of morphine.

Reversing the effects

The next major discovery came in the 1950s, when researchers found that by slightly changing an opioid molecule they could produce a drug which antagonised (blocked) or reversed the effects of opioid drugs. The first obvious use of such drugs was in the treatment of overdoses of opioid drugs. These antagonists were later used as starting points in the search for pain-relieving drugs that would not produce 'addiction' or drug-seeking behaviour. This search has had some success in that there are now drugs that appear to be less likely than others to lead to dependence. However, until very recently, scientists had no clear idea of just how the opioids did what they did in the body.

It was between 1973 and 1975 that several groups of researchers, including Candice Pert and Solomon Snyder, Eric Simon and Lars Terenius, independently published papers revealing that they had isolated specific sites or 'receptors' on nerve cells with which the opioid drugs interacted. The 'opioid receptor' was found only on certain nerve cells in the body and only in vertebrate organisms. For instance, there are no opioid receptors in the clam, the octopus or the earthworm. Researchers puzzled over the reasons for the presence of these receptors. One obvious possibility was that they were receptors for some as yet undiscovered substance that is naturally present within the brain.

This view was confirmed in 1975, when John Hughes and Hans Kosterlitz of Aberdeen isolated from the brain of the rat two molecules which acted like opioids: they combined with the opioid receptors, produced opioid effects and were antagonised by opioid antagonists. Hughes and his co-workers named these naturally occurring opioid substances 'enkephalins'. Other workers soon confirmed this finding, and Avram Goldstein and his co-workers in Palo Alto, California, found in the pituitary gland of the pig a larger peptide molecule—called β-endorphin—which also had a powerful opioid action. Within months it became clear that the enkephalins were distributed in nervous tissue in a manner almost identical to that of the opioid receptors. The evidence pointed overwhelmingly to the fact that the enkephalins were transmitter substances produced by neurons to influence the actions of other neurons by combining with the opioid receptors. The opioid family of drugs acted by mimicking the actions of the naturally occurring substances.[2]

These remarkable discoveries have cast some light on how opioids induce physical dependence. But we are still a long way from understanding why some people find the effects of these drugs so gratifying that their use comes to control their lives. The discovery of endogenous opioids does, however, raise the possibility that some people find the opioids especially satisfying and seem to relapse repeatedly after withdrawal because of an imbalance in the opioid systems of their brains.

Feeling high

The effects of the opioid drugs on mood and feelings depend on the situation (the setting), the previous experiences and expectations of the person taking the drug (the set), the amount

'I can't get no satisfaction. . .' but the addicts of rock do!

taken, and the route of administration (whether the drug is taken by mouth, inhaled, or injected intravenously). Former heroin addicts say that opioids produce a pleasurable 'high'. There is a general indifference to threatening situations ('it makes my troubles roll off my mind') and, in some cases, increased energy and a sense of unusual wellbeing (euphoria). These effects probably result from action at receptors in the emotion centres in the brain. Addicts also describe a special sensation—a 'thrill' or 'rush' lasting for about a minute immediately after injecting the drug intravenously.

Interestingly, physicians and nurses who become dependent on opioids describe the subjective effects in almost the same way. After as little as a few weeks of regular use, the duration of the euphoria becomes quite short and the overall mood becomes almost or slightly depressed. Tolerance and physical dependence to opioids can develop to a significant degree within this short space of time.[3]

Opioid withdrawal

The opioid withdrawal syndrome in its severe form consists of a number of effects that seem to be the opposite of those produced by the drug itself. These include anxiety, sleeplessness, increased sensitivity to pain, nausea, vomiting, fever, sweating, kicking movements, abdominal cramps and diarrhoea. All of these are quickly relieved by taking an opioid drug.

This combination of symptoms may seem awful, yet the opioids are not as destructive to the organs of the body as is alcohol. When the drugs are taken by mouth (as in methadone maintenance programmes), tolerance develops. Regular users may enjoy relatively good health, normal psychological functioning and lead a law-abiding, productive life. This does not mean that someone taking large doses of opioids is completely normal physiologically. There is not complete tolerance to all the opioid effects. Constipation may be a problem, and the function of endocrine glands (for instance sex glands) may be depressed.[3]

The risks—and those who take them

Not all opioid users take the drugs by mouth. When opioids are injected intravenously, there is always a danger of potentially fatal infections. When injected under the skin, some opioids destroy the tissues; when smoked there is damage to the lungs. But perhaps the major reason for concern about continued opioid use is that many users seem unwilling to accept the inevitable loss of the euphoric (i.e. antidepressant) effects. They keep increasing the dose to try to recapture these effects—even briefly. Eventually they find that their lives are like roller-coasters—brief periods of normality or even 'euphoria' punctuated by longer periods of thinking about the avoidance of withdrawal which recurs each time the drug effects wear off.

Two groups of people have relatively easy access to low cost opioids—physicians, who can take them from the supplies intended for patients, and those who grow opium or live in countries where its purchase is legal.

Some physicians are able to take opioids such as morphine and continue to practise with relatively little impairment. Their drug use is undetected by patients or other doctors. Some opium smokers in countries that permit legal purchase of opium seem able to carry out their responsibilities reasonably well. Yet there are other physicians and opium smokers who reach the point where the drug effect dominates their lives. Work is neglected or performed so poorly that they are coerced into treatment by family or friends.

Against the law

In most countries of the world, opioids are not available for 'recreational' use. Those who want an opioid 'high' must buy their drug (usually heroin) from an illicit source at high prices. Is it the high price and the illegality of the drug that leads to the picture of the urban 'junkie' (heroin addict), unable or unwilling to work and getting enough money to buy heroin by stealing or selling drugs? The answer is far from simple.

When a drug is both illegal and socially disapproved of, those who try it are more likely to come from a delinquent background; at the least, they are unconventional and unconcerned about social sanctions. As noted in Chapter 2 many are depressed and have low self-esteem.

In the United States, more than half of those who are identified as heroin addicts had a history of delinquent behaviour or a criminal conviction before they first used heroin. The figure is similar in Great Britain, even though there are clinics that provide heroin to established addicts. On the other hand, there are some people who have no criminal involvement and lead relatively conventional lives (working, raising families), despite their use of illegal heroin.

It was clearly shown in a study of English heroin addicts by Gerry Stimpson that even when heroin is provided by clinics, the diversity of behaviour persists. Some are law-abiding, using only what is prescribed; some users subsist on welfare; some sell drugs; and still others steal and buy extra heroin on the black market.[4] It seems clear that providing free drugs to heroin users who are committed to criminal activity as a way of life will lower their cost of living and reduce crime to an extent, but it will not eliminate it.

Somewhere in the crowd there's always someone who's got what you want—if you can pay the price.

Once an addict, not always an addict

It is far from easy, but not impossible, to give up the use of opioids once the learning and conditioning processes (described in Chapter 2) have occurred. Even under the best of economic conditions, such as one might see among addicted physicians, the chance of a first time long-term success is not high. Many relapse after a period of abstinence.

One common factor in relapse is the continued presence of some emotional disorder such as depression which the former addict again seeks to relieve with the drug. But there are times when the reasons for relapse seem obscure, and it is apparently

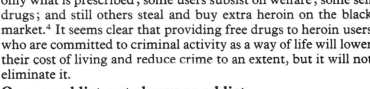

due to a sharp increase in craving coinciding with the availability of the drug.

But the chances of giving up opioid use increase over the longer term. Follow-up studies of heroin addicts registered at London clinics found that, regardless of the specific treatment received, a substantial proportion (about one third) were functioning well and using neither opioids nor any other drug to excess. However, about half were still using opioids obtained from clinics, others were in prison, and the death rate (mostly from overdoses) was about 1·5 per cent per year, many times greater than might be expected for a comparison population of similar age.[5] These findings are also seen among heroin addicts who were treated in the United States, despite the different legal situation.[6] The most significant difference between the two countries is that among American addicts a higher proportion of the deaths are due to homicide and suicide.

What makes it possible for one opioid addict to recover while another continues drug use, and still another becomes a statistic in the mortality tables? If we ask the former addicts themselves, they are likely to attribute it to some change in their lives— something good happening, the love or the trust of a specific person. Perhaps they find the reasons for changing more powerful than those for continuing.

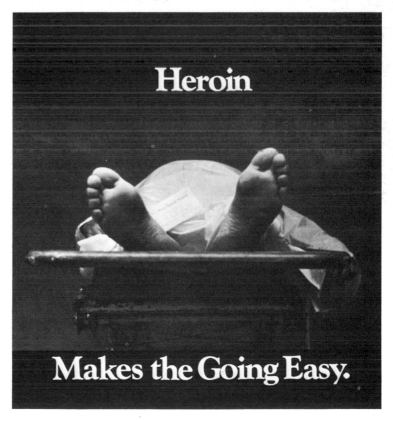

Heroin

Makes the Going Easy.

... but how do you come back?

4   Looking for a lift

When coffee and tea were introduced into Western societies in the 17th century they provided a new possibility for modifying mood. Before that time, there were drugs like alcohol and opium to produce sedation and calming but none to alleviate fatigue and lift the spirits. These two sociable beverages were the first anti-fatigue and mood-elevating drugs available to Europeans.

At first, coffee elicited many of the same cries of moral outrage as had greeted the introduction of tobacco 40 or 50 years previously—and from the same people. But by the time tea (*bohea* or *chah*, as it was called) came along (in 1657 in Britain) acceptance was readier. Coffee and tea soon became an influential part of the fabric of respectable society. They also rapidly established themselves as economically important trading crops, and contributed a great deal to the development of commercial navigation.[4]

In the United States and Western Europe, the caffeine in coffee and tea was the only stimulant available until *coca* preparations and *cocaine* were introduced in the late 19th century. But within less than 25 years, concern about the dependence potential and toxic effects of cocaine led to severe restrictions on its use. It is therefore not surprising to find that history has much less to say about the use and abuse of stimulants than about that of alcohol and opiates. Not until the 1930s were the amphetamines, the most powerful of synthetic stimulants, introduced into medicine; and it was another decade before they appeared outside the clinics as a widespread drug of abuse.

Speed can kill . . .

The amphetamines are a family of drugs that, when given in the usual therapeutic doses, produce an elevation of mood, a decrease in fatigue, and lowering of appetite. There is also a reduced need for sleep. Some people, given amphetamines even at therapeutic doses, seem more irritable and more talkative.

At present it is believed that these drugs work by releasing the transmitter substances *noradrenaline* and *dopamine* from nerve endings. But it was for one of their incidental effects that amphetamines were first introduced to the public. They were

How high can you go?

used in nasal inhalers because they produce a constriction of blood vessels and, in this way, relieve the stuffy nose that accompanies the common cold. Benzedrine (an early trade name for amphetamine) was also found to be extremely helpful in treating narcolepsy, a rare disorder in which the victim falls asleep spontaneously and unpredictably during normal waking hours. It was also found effective in treating children who exhibit extreme restlessness and distractability that causes learning and behaviour problems. In these children, who are sometimes called 'hyperactive' and whom some experts believe have 'minimal brain damage', amphetamines and certain related drugs (e.g. methylphenadate) have the paradoxical effect of markedly reducing the hyperactivity and the inability to focus attention. Amphetamines are sometimes used to treat mild depression, although their usefulness for this purpose has been seriously questioned.

Fighting fatigue and fat

During the Second World War, amphetamines were given to pilots and other combat personnel to reduce the need for sleep. Under both laboratory and real-life conditions these drugs prevent the performance-sapping drowsiness and fatigue which normally accompany long hours of continuous performance under arduous conditions. At the end of the war, the Japanese released large stockpiles of amphetamines which had been developed for wartime use. This increased availability was a major factor in the post-war 'epidemic' of amphetamine abuse that swept Japan.[1] Amphetamines still play a role in alleviating fatigue: they were given to American astronauts to help them to cope with the demands and dangers of space flight.

Perhaps the most widespread and, currently, the most controversial use of amphetamines is in the treatment of obesity. Because they suppress appetite, amphetamines can help patients to lose weight. Tolerance to this appetite-suppressing effect usually develops within a matter of eight to twelve weeks, so that the use of amphetamines for any longer gives no help with a diet. But some doctors continue to prescribe and dispense amphetamines for periods of months or years under the guise of treating obesity. The use of amphetamines for this purpose has been sharply attacked, and several countries—Britain is one—have outlawed their use for all purposes other than the treatment of narcolepsy and hyperactivity in children.

Patterns of abuse

A drug which produces an elevated mood and enables its user to feel more competent, more energetic, more capable of sustained effort is a natural candidate for abuse. Since they first appeared the amphetamines have been extensively used for non-medical purposes. Several patterns of abuse have been seen.

*Busy busy busy...
stimulants can help
you keep up a frantic
pace—for a while.*

In one, relatively small amounts are used either on one occasion or on a more regular basis. Users of this type include college students cramming all night for examinations, long distance truck drivers, busy executives intent on working longer or harder, housewives who discover that diet pills give them a lift in mood and make them feel able to face the day and get their tasks done. These people generally keep the dosage at moderate or low levels, and their use of the drug may be viewed as functional. The big danger in this pattern is that the user will come to feel an increasing need to take the drug in order to maintain the good feeling or to avoid the 'let-down' when the drug is stopped.

Because tolerance to the mood-elevating and appetite-suppressing effects of the drug develops, it often requires somewhat larger doses to maintain the effect the user obtained originally with small doses. In some cases, the sense of enhanced capacity produced by the drug comes to be viewed as essential. When attempts are made to stop, the user finds himself 'bogged down' or depressed. When they increase the dose, some users begin to experience increased irritability, tremulousness, inability to sleep and suspiciousness about other people's motives. Amphetamines may also cause a compulsive talkativeness and grinding of the teeth. More rarely, this type of user may develop a serious mental disorder with characteristics very like those of paranoid schizophrenia.

A second, more pernicious pattern of abuse is that of the so-called 'speed freak'. The term 'speed' is sometimes used to refer to methamphetamine (a close relative of amphetamine) and sometimes to all members of the amphetamine family. As part of this second pattern of abuse, large amounts of amphetamine may be injected intravenously, with the dose repeated very often over the course of a 'run' of several days. The consequences can be disastrous.

31

Epidemics of intravenous amphetamine abuse have occurred in several parts of the world. The one in post-war Japan may have involved several million people, and an epidemic in Scandinavia between 1965 and 1968 involved the release of an amphetamine related drug (phenmetrazine) without controls on to the market. At much the same time a similar epidemic occurred in the United States, primarily in California, and there have been sporadic outbursts among smaller numbers of people in many parts of the world.[1,2]

Picture of a speed freak

The development and characteristics of the typical 'speed freak' have been described by John Kramer and others.[1] He or she has usually experimented with a number of drugs, including oral amphetamines. The first use of the intravenous 'speed' (unlike the first use of most other drugs) is an 'ecstatic' experience. Initial use of the drug is intermittent, in doses of 20–40mg per injection, once or several times over one or two days. Days, even weeks, may intervene between the initial drug-injecting sprees. Gradually, however, the periods of drug use become longer, the drug-free period shorter, the doses higher and the injections more frequent.

After a period of some months, the user injects many times a day in quantities as high as 100 times the dose that could be taken by a non-tolerant individual on a single occasion. He or she remains awake for from three to six days or longer, becoming more and more tense, tremulous and ultimately paranoid as the 'run' continues. Between periods of such intense use, the user falls exhausted ('crashes') into a profound sleep lasting as long as 48 hours, only to repeat the cycle on awakening.

Immediately following each injection the user may experience an intensely ecstatic, euphoric sensation ('the flash') in which he or she feels extremely adequate, capable, brimming over with energy and wellbeing. This has been described as 'a maximal stimulus to the pleasure centre of the brain'.[2] Over time, this ecstatic experience becomes more elusive. It requires larger and larger doses to produce the desired effect and to avoid intense fatigue and depression which ultimately ensues.

Because very large doses of amphetamines profoundly reduce appetite, even the act of eating becomes repugnant. In extreme cases, malnutrition results. Weight loss, loss of sleep, extreme stimulation from the drug and other illnesses to which users are susceptible combine to make the user appear wasted and significantly older than his or her chronological age.

When animals with implanted intravenous catheters are given continuous access to amphetamines, they behave like 'speed freaks': they will repeatedly press a lever for an injection; they develop obvious toxicity and appear to be hallucinating; they chew at their own limbs, and they stop eating. But they manage to continue pressing the lever. Death in these animals usually supervenes in a matter of weeks.

Psychological deterioration

Not street theatre but real tragedy in the street.

It is known that prolonged sleep loss alone can produce seriously disordered thinking. But there is good reason to believe that the amphetamines themselves induce psychotic thinking and behaviour. By giving repeated doses of these drugs (in much smaller doses than the typical 'speed freak' uses) to normal male volunteers, a group of researchers in the United States were able to produce symptoms like those of acute schizophrenia.

The symptoms described were strikingly like those reported by street users: suspicions that others were talking about them or plotting against them, irritability, sometimes accompanied by marked hostility, aggressive behaviour, marked grandiosity, belief in the profound significance of the user's thoughts, auditory and olfactory hallucinations and occasionally persistent sexual arousal (priapism).[3]

Another striking feature of the toxic drug state is repetitive behaviour—polishing a car for many hours, arranging possessions or cleaning a house to a point of inhuman perfection. That this is somehow caused by the drug itself is suggested by animal experiments in which the animals show similar repetitive stereotyped behaviour, characteristic of their own species, when given large doses of amphetamines.

Despite the American hippie slogan 'Speed kills', death from the drug itself is not common. Death from other hazards of the user's lifestyle is more likely. There may be violent confrontation with an imagined adversary or the police, serum hepatitis (from using non-sterile needles), endocarditis (inflammation of the membrane surrounding the heart), blood clots in veins and abcesses at injection sites, septicaemia from the use of impure drugs clandestinely manufactured.

Even when the 'speed freak' has entered the schizophrenia-like state, he or she will usually completely recover from the effects of the drug after several drug-free months.[3] There is a tendency to relapse because of the fatigue and depression of the withdrawal reaction, and outside restraints are often necessary to keep the 'speeder' off the drug. After a number of years, however, a substantial percentage of users give up drug use, or turn to more conventional substances such as alcohol.

Other stimulants?

While the amphetamines are the most commonly abused of the stimulant drugs, other chemically and pharmacologically similar

33

drugs are also abused. Two of these are phenmetrazine (sold as Preludin for appetite control in the United States) and methylphenidate (marketed under the trade name Ritalin).

Methylphenidate, in legitimate medical use, is prescribed for mild depression, narcolepsy, for hyperactive children and apathetic elderly patients who are socially withdrawn from others. In illicit use, its effects are generally similar to those of the other stimulants. However, the effects of intravenous injection are likely to be more severe since the tablets contain talcum as a binder. This frequently causes inflammation of the veins as well as scarring of blood vessels. Phenmetrazine, popular as a drug of abuse in Sweden (where there were at one time 10,000 estimated users in a population of eight million) is much like the amphetamines in its effects.

Uppers and downers together

Simultaneous use of both sedatives and stimulants is not only possible but extremely common. The habitual user of even modest doses of amphetamines frequently feels the need to 'unwind' by means of a depressant. The 'speed' user may also feel a need for a depressant to reduce the extreme tremulousness resulting from his use of 'speed', or to help him 'crash' at the end of a run. Many individuals switch among a variety of drugs, depending on availability and the impulse of the moment. Such polydrug abuse complicates drug treatment and subsequent recovery.

It is useful to recall that terms like 'uppers' and 'downers', 'stimulant' and 'depressant' are very crude descriptions of what the drugs really do. In reality they do not have opposite effects.

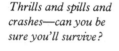

Thrills and spills and crashes—can you be sure you'll survive?

Who uses stimulants?

Large-scale surveys which have been conducted in the United States since 1971 have shown that the non-medical use of amphetamines is not uncommon. In 1977, ten per cent of adolescents reported having at some time used a stimulant. Among young adults, 21 per cent had used stimulants, but only about 2·5 per cent reported having used the drugs in the month prior to the interview. The incidence of dependence—regular heavy use—can be presumed to be smaller still.

Among adolescents using or experimenting with amphetamines, a recurring theme is the previous use of more conventional (less deviant) drugs. They are usually cigarette smokers, drink alcohol, and are generally users of marihuana. While some users of stimulants may go on to experiment with LSD and opiates (which are viewed by society and their own peers as even more deviant), others will stop at stimulants and sedatives—uppers and downers.

Initial use of stimulants comes about in the usual way for almost all drugs—availability and peer group convention play an important part. But additional psychological factors may also be important. While showing more risk-taking, more anti-conventional attitudes, amphetamine users are also more alienated from the values of the dominant culture. They often have greater strains in their family relationships and even lower expectations of what conventional scholastic activities will bring.

Keeping Saturday night at fever pitch.

Psychological studies of the 'speed freak' and of individuals who are hospitalised for amphetamine psychosis generally reveal a great deal of psychopathology preceding the use of the drug. A significant proportion had alcohol problems and had been in trouble with the law, and some had family backgrounds in which alcoholism, criminality and serious mental illness were prominent features.

The ultimate high

Cocaine, with its romantic history and its high cost, is regarded by drug users as *the* status drug. Although, when injected intravenously in the laboratory, human subjects have trouble distinguishing it from the more pedestrian amphetamines, it remains the Rolls-Royce of illicit drugs.

Unlike the other stimulants discussed, cocaine is a naturally occurring substance, extracted from the leaves of the South American coca shrub (*Erythroxylon coca*). These leaves have been chewed since antiquity by Indians in the Andes for their fatigue-dispelling and stimulant properties. Their use was originally (about 800 AD) the highly esteemed privilege of the nobles of the Peruvian Inca Empire. Legend has it that the god Inti instructed the moon mother, Mama Quilla, to plant coca in the humid valleys of the Andes in order to mitigate the hunger and thirst of the Incas so that they would be better able to endure earthly demands. But by the time of the Spanish conquest (1536), coca had lost much of its high symbolic significance.

The leaf that refreshed
The attitude of the Spanish conquerors towards coca was decidedly mixed. On the one hand their religious zeal dictated that they eliminate this persistent symbol of Incan idolatry. But they also realised that coca enabled the Indians to work harder in the mines and elsewhere, making it an important economic asset. In the end, the latter consideration prevailed. Coca cultivation, distribution and use was permitted—even encouraged— as one means of economically exploiting a subjugated people.

Reports about this energising and euphoria-producing substance did not take long to reach the Old World. Moreover, the widespread use of coca as an Indian folk medicine (which continues to this day) led Spanish physicians to advocate its use for such diverse purposes as the treatment of stomach disorders, headache, muscular pains, skin ulcerations and 'weakness'.

Despite the obvious importance of coca to the Incas and the early recognition of its economic and medicinal value by the Spanish, it was not until 1750 that the first plant specimens were sent to Europe for systematic study.[4,5] Coca attracted little serious medical or scientific attention outside Spain until the latter half of the 19th century. There were two reasons for this: the plant was not well suited for growing in Europe, and the imported leaves had usually lost most of their pharmacological properties on the long sea journey.

But in 1860 Albert Niemann, in Germany, isolated from coca leaves a new substance which he named 'cocaine'. He had created a new and powerful drug capable of exciting the most profound initial enthusiasm and, later, an equally profound dread.

Medical use and abuse

When cocaine became available, there was an era of great medical excitement over the drug's therapeutic potential. Sigmund Freud, then a young neurologist, was one of cocaine's most prominent investigators. Inspired by preliminary American and German accounts of its use for the treatment of fatigue and of alcohol and morphine addiction, Freud eagerly experimented with the new stimulant. Making personal as well as therapeutic use of it, he soon became uncritically enthusiastic. He wrote a major paper, *On Coca*, in which he advocated the use of cocaine for treating digestive disorders, asthma, so-called wasting diseases (such as cancer), as an aphrodisiac, a general stimulant and as a local anaesthetic. It was as a local anaesthetic, specifically in eye surgery, that it became most important in Freud's time.

But with medical use came abuse. Ernst von Fleischl, a friend and colleague of Freud's, had become morphine dependent as a result of the treatment of an old injury and sought his help. Freud recommended cocaine. The switch from morphine to cocaine was readily made, but in a short time von Fleischl was taking larger and larger doses, which culminated in what may have been the first cocaine psychosis.

The symptoms he showed are still typical of the disorder—acute mental illness like that of *delirium tremens* in alcoholism, with hallucinations that worms, snakes and other vermin were burrowing beneath the surface of his skin. Like others since, von Fleischl excoriated his flesh in an effort to dig out the 'invaders'. His thinking became quite paranoid and he remained seriously disturbed until his death some years later. Freud, who thought cocaine a very safe drug, was later also inadvertently to kill a patient with an overdose.

With the rise in adverse psychological effects like those experienced by von Fleischl and amidst mounting reports of medically induced accidental deaths from the new drug, the enthusiasm of physicians for cocaine became more muted. Freud himself was derided by Erlenmeyer, an authority on addiction, for having unleashed 'the third scourge of humanity' (alcohol and the opiates being the other two).

A cure-all for the masses

The last two decades of the 19th century were the climax of the patent medicine era. The initial enthusiasm of some of the medical profession for cocaine was uncritical, and the eagerness

*Things go better...
even without the
cocaine, the
attraction of Coca-
Cola has remained.*

with which patent medicine purveyors seized on the new
stimulant was still more so. Cocaine became part of such tonic
wines as *Vin Mariani* and of hundreds of other nostrums. It was
even for a time (until 1903) an ingredient of a newly developed
American soft drink destined for worldwide fame, Coca Cola.[1]

In America as well as in Europe, however, the coming of age
of scientifically based medicine and of the pharmaceutical
industry led to new demands for higher ethical standards and to
increased concern about the implications of the indiscriminate
use of such substances as opium and cocaine. New regulations
were passed. The combination of increasingly adverse publicity
about the 'cocaine habit' together with the new restrictions led
to a marked decline in both medical and recreational use.

Today it has two main medical uses: it is still used in nose-
throat surgery because of its unique properties as an excellent
local anaesthetic and as an agent which contracts blood vessels,
reducing bleeding at the operation site. Its widest present use
may be as an ingredient in the Brompton Cocktail. This a
combination of alcohol, heroin or morphine and cocaine which
is used as a painkiller and tonic for patients with terminal cancer.

Cocaine abuse today

It was the youth counter-culture of the 1960s, especially in the
United States, which adopted such drugs as marijuana and LSD.
Some authorities believe that the drugs were valued almost as
much as symbols of protest as for their pharmacological effects.
With the rise in interest in those drugs came a renewed interest
in cocaine. The use of this drug has recently increased markedly,
especially among young adults in the United States. National

survey statistics in 1977 indicated that one in five 18- to 25-year-olds had tried the stimulant. Even among American secondary seniors (aged 17–18) one in every nine members reported having tried cocaine. Most such use is, however, more aptly termed experimental than habitual. Less than one in five of those in the 18–25 age group reported having used the drug in the previous month.[5]

What cocaine does for you

Perhaps more than any other stimulant drug, users believe cocaine produces an intense euphoria, a sense of strong stimulation and of profound wellbeing. When experienced drug users are asked to rank drugs for personal desirability, they almost invariably rank cocaine first. In the laboratory animals given the opportunity to self-inject drugs by means of implanted intravenous catheters, cocaine is the most powerful reinforcer known. Animals put on a fixed ratio schedule so that many lever presses are required to obtain a dose of cocaine will press more than 6,000 times for a single dose. Its reputation as the 'ultimate high', its widespread reported use by some celebrities, even its high cost, all combine to make its use appealing. And, because of its high cost and its limited availability, seriously adverse consequences are probably less common than with other stimulants. However, animals given unlimited access to cocaine continue to press a lever until they develop severe toxicity. They usually stop eating, often chew at their own limbs, and usually die in a matter of weeks.

Most users snort 'coke', inhaling the fine crystalline powder into the nose by means of a straw or a rolled up piece of paper currency. Deposited on the nasal mucous membranes, the drug is rapidly and efficiently absorbed into the bloodstream. Because the effects of the drug are of short duration (as little as half an hour or less), the user must repeatedly snort 'lines' of the finely divided crystalline material if the 'high' is to be maintained.[5]

Intravenous injection of a liquid cocaine solution is also possible, but is less common. Unlike such drugs as heroin, LSD or even marijuana, cocaine does not usually result in a 'turning inward'. Instead, users see it as a 'social drug' which facilitates social interaction somewhat like low doses of alcohol. As with other psychoactive drugs, however, cocaine's effects are likely to be influenced by the user's personality and expectations, as well as by the social and physical environment in which the drug is taken.

The most obvious physiological effect, as with other stimulants, is an increase in heart rate and in blood pressure. Since the drug tends to constrict blood vessels, its repeated use by inhalation may injure the mucous membranes of the nose. Frequent users may develop symptoms like those of a head cold, perhaps further aggravated by the chronic use of nasal sprays to make breathing easier.

Subjectively reported effects include the universally acknowledged euphoria and general feeling of wellbeing, the 'high' already described, reduced tiredness, diminished appetite, garrulousness and, in a small minority of users, sexual stimulation and increased sociability. Less pleasant effects reported by groups of regular users include restlessness, anxiety, overexcitability, irritability and, for some, paranoid feelings.

With heavier, more frequent use, as with other stimulants, users begin to report skin reactions ranging from itchiness to the sensation some kind of parasite is moving under the skin. Increased hearing acuity and awareness of smells occurs, which begins to border on or include auditory and olfactory hallucinations (hearing persistent whispering, for example, or others calling one's name; things 'smell bad').

She knows how. . .
a tube of paper is
used to inhale
cocaine.

Cocaine psychosis

With still heavier, daily use of cocaine, a cocaine psychosis sometimes occurs which is similar to that resulting from prolonged amphetamine abuse. It has also been described as closely resembling paranoid schizophrenia. The itching skin sensations already alluded to become further intensified to become feelings that insects, worms or other parasites are burrowing in the skin. They become sufficiently vivid for the user to tear at his or her skin in a frantic effort to rid it of the imagined invaders.

The user also loses insight into the drug-induced nature of the syndrome and believes that he or she is being persecuted or threatened. As with the amphetamines, heavier, more frequent use leading to this type of thinking may be accompanied by violent behaviour in response to the 'threat'. In contrast to the careful studies of amphetamine psychosis, cocaine psychosis has not been systematically studied under laboratory conditions and so it is not known just what frequency of use and how much of the drug are likely to cause it.[4, 5]

Peril or panacea?

There is a widespread belief among cocaine users that the drug is relatively harmless. Its high cost and limited availability have undoubtedly contributed to that belief. Supporters of this view sometimes point to the relatively benign effects of coca leaf chewing by Indians in the Andes. But this disregards the important differences in effect that go with an alteration in the route of administration: direct absorption (by 'snorting' or injection) will produce stronger reactions than the ingestion, over the time of chewing, of the low concentration of the drug in the coca leaf. In parts of Latin America where purified cocaine is readily available at a relatively low cost, the incidence of serious adverse effects is much higher than in Europe and North America.

Deaths resulting from cocaine overdoses are not common and usually occur as a result of having swallowed a container of cocaine in order to smuggle it across international borders. It is assumed that death occurs when the swallowed container breaks, spilling the contents in large quantity. Occasionally a user who snorts or injects the drug may kill himself through overdose since there are large differences in drug sensitivity among users.[5]

5 Down with anxiety

For centuries physicians have been searching for ways to calm the troubled, anxious patient and to restore the luxury of sleep to the sleepless. But until the 19th century, the medicines available to accomplish this were limited largely to substances derived from opium, or to the use of preparations containing alcohol. While some additional depressants—the bromide salts, paraldehyde, and chloral hydrate— became available in the 19th century, all had serious disadvantages. Bromides were relatively ineffective and their use even in the short term carried the risk of bromide poisoning. Chloral hydrate and paraldehyde are objectionable, among other reasons, for their decidedly unpleasant taste and smell. Thus, when barbituric acid derivatives became available shortly after the end of the 19th century, they were hailed as great advances over earlier sedative-hypnotics.

They were stable and uniform in potency and could be synthesised in long-acting and shorter-acting forms, as well as in combinations of the two, to meet a variety of medical needs. Depending on the dose, this large family of related sedative-hypnotic drugs can be used in a number of ways. They can produce sedation and relaxation, decrease anxiety, induce sleep, and raise the threshold for epileptic seizures. Certain barbiturates can be used as anaesthetics, since in high dosage they induce unconsciousness.

However, reports of the use of barbiturates to produce alcohol-like intoxication followed within a few years of their first use, and the observation that some people were using them on a regular basis soon followed. By 1927 scientists had found that barbital is habit forming 'beyond a question of a doubt.'

Despite such reports, despite the demonstration that they induced severe physical dependence, and despite the evidence that they were becoming a favourite means of committing suicide in the United States, the barbiturates remained readily available, until the 1960s, on prescriptions that could be refilled repeatedly and indefinitely.

What, me worry?

Barbiturate abuse

Several distinct patterns of barbiturate abuse and dependence became apparent. Some users resemble the 'delta alcoholic': they never appear to be intoxicated, yet they ingest high doses of sedative-hypnotic drugs on a daily basis and seem unable to do without them. Included in this group are many people such as housewives and businessmen who originally obtained the drugs from physicians for the treatment of anxiety or insomnia, and in time increased the dose. Often, the drug is mainly used at night to induce sleep. Eventually, however, dependence reaches a point where it is necessary to take small doses during the day to prevent withdrawal symptoms.

Another group of users resembles the 'gamma alcoholic'. These people use the drugs deliberately to induce intoxication, often on 'binges'. Some may obtain their drugs from physicians, but more often they buy them illegally.

Some of those who use sedative-hypnotics in this way and have become physically dependent on them also have alcohol-related problems. They may have been problem drinkers or alcoholics before starting to use barbiturates. Such people may use these drugs in either of the two patterns described above, and they may obtain them from either of the two sources described. In addition, many heroin users may also use barbiturates to 'boost' the effect of diluted street drugs.[1]

Search for alternatives

Efforts were made to find substitutes free of the liabilities of the barbiturates. This led to the introduction of a dozen or more drugs which, while technically and chemically not barbiturates (since they were not based on the basic barbiturate molecule), had virtually all of their properties—including, as it has turned out, the drawbacks. In appropriate doses, they all produce sedation and sleep; but they also produce a barbiturate-alcohol type of euphoria or 'high' in larger doses.

Reports of abuse quickly followed the introduction of each, and it became apparent that they induced a similar physical dependence. Within limits, they were effectively interchangeable with barbiturates in all uses. Today they are all considered to be pharmacologically related to sedative-hypnotics and, in most countries, are required to carry warning labels and subjected to legal regulations.

There is still controversy about the classification of the benzodiazepine family of drugs, the best known members of which are Librium, Valium, and Dalmane. These drugs—the minor tranquillisers or anti-anxiety agents—produce a decrease in anxiety, induce sleep, raise seizure thresholds, and, in very large doses, produce coma. They are in general longer-acting than barbiturates, produce less euphoria on acute ingestion, and are less likely to cause death even when large doses are deliberately ingested. Because of these advantages, the benzodiazepines are rapidly displacing the older sedative-hypnotics for almost every use except intravenous anaesthesia.[1]

Why depress yourself?

It is not altogether clear just why these sedative hypnotic drugs are misused—that is, used in ways and in doses that physicians do not approve of. Whatever the reasons, they and the anti-anxiety agents, while of undeniable medical usefulness, are also important drugs of abuse. In developed countries, the problem probably exceeds that of opioid abuse in extent, if not in its adverse social consequences.

Drugs in this class are strikingly similar in their subjective and physiological effects to alcohol. This has been found to be true in street use, as well as in the more carefully controlled conditions of the laboratory. In the 1950s, scientists at the Addiction Research Center in Lexington, Kentucky, systematically demonstrated the similarity of the effects of high doses of barbiturates and of alcohol, including their tendency to produce dependence and severe withdrawal symptoms.

As is the case with other psychoactive drugs, the effects of the depressants are heavily dependent on the 'set' and 'setting' of the use (see Chapter 1) as well as on the dose and route of administration. There are also large differences in how people react to these drugs, and in the ease with which they become dependent on them.[2]

What is a lethal dose?

Tolerance develops to the sedative hypnotics, but the pattern is quite different from that seen with opioid drugs. Someone tolerant to sedatives is often able to function with considerable amounts of the drug in the body, but there is a relatively low upper limit to the tolerance. It is thus quite easy to achieve a state of intoxication, or deliberately or accidentally to ingest a fatal overdose of the drug.

It is estimated that even in very tolerant individuals, the lethal dose of barbiturates may be less than twice the dose that would kill a non-tolerant person. A considerable degree of cross-tolerance also exists between the sedative-hypnotics: an individual tolerant to pentobarbital, for example, would also be tolerant to chemically distinct but pharmacologically similar drugs such as methaqualone, glutethimide, or chloral hydrate. Cross-tolerance between the barbiturates and the benzodiazepines (such as Valium and Librium) also develops.[2]

Physical dependence

In some respects, physical dependence on barbiturate-like drugs is more serious than dependence on opioids. In the very dependent person (someone taking more than 800mg per day of pentobarbital or its equivalent dose of other drugs), abrupt withdrawal of the drug produces a syndrome beginning with anxiety, shakiness, weakness, and insomnia. Within 24 hours or less (the onset is much delayed with drugs that are slowly excreted), the syndrome may progress to convulsions and a delirium which resembles the *delirium tremens* (DTs) seen in alcoholic withdrawal. There is often a rapid heart rate, fever, confusion and hallucinations. Deaths have been reported to occur following abrupt withdrawal of sedative-hypnotics in heavily dependent people.

The long dark night of the soul.

Overdoses and toxicity

Another problem commonly associated with the excessive use of 'downers' is accidental overdosage. In the most common circumstances, someone who has had a number of alcoholic drinks at a party returns home and takes a barbiturate tablet to ensure a good night's sleep. Minutes later, he or she forgets having taken the earlier dose and takes another.

The extra dosage of barbiturate combines with the alcohol already consumed to depress breathing to the point where death results. The combination of alcohol with sedative-hypnotics is particularly dangerous because the simultaneous action of the two drugs is not only additive but synergistic (each accentuates the other's action). Jointly, they depress the brain and also inhibit the mechanisms responsible for getting drugs out of the body. Even alone, barbiturates are among the most favoured drugs for suicidal overdoses, which often succeed since their action is rapid and profound.

Periodically, new drugs are introduced that are thought to be safer. Methaqualone, sold in the United States as Quaalude and Sopor and in other countries as Mandrax, was once heralded for its alleged safety and for its lack of dependence liability, especially compared to the barbiturates. It is now evident that it, too, can produce dependence and, combined with alcohol, can also be life-endangering. Excessive doses can produce coma; after withdrawal, convulsions are sometimes seen.

The sedative-hypnotics have an undeserved reputation among street users as aphrodisiacs—drugs which accentuate sexual desire. But, like alcohol, while they may reduce inhibitions and thereby apparently make the user more sexually aggressive, in larger doses they are actually likely to interfere with sexual performance (See Chapter 9, on alcohol).

A world on 'downers'

Sedative-hypnotic drugs are used in every society that has access to modern pharmaceuticals. Cases of abuse and dependence are common in most Western countries and have been reported in

Every day the world's population consumes truckloads of pills.

countries in South East Asia and Africa as well. While it is difficult to gauge the extent of use and dependence among those who obtain the drugs illicitly, a fairly systematic household survey in the United States revealed that, in 1977, six per cent of all adults aged 18 and over had used a sedative drug that had not been prescribed, and 4·8 per cent of adults had used some kind of tranquilliser, as distinct from sedatives. Among people between the ages of 18 and 25, the proportion reporting non-medical use of sedatives jumped to more than 18 per cent. Another 13 per cent reported the use of tranquillisers not prescribed for any particular medical treatment. During the same year, nearly 20 per cent of adults reported experience with sedatives in a medical context, and nine per cent reported that they had used them during the previous year. More than one adult in three reported having used a tranquilliser at some time, with about one in six reporting use during the previous year.

Such household surveys do not provide a good index of problems that may be related to the use of sedative drugs. But numerous studies suggest that the more extensive the use, the more likely it is that some people will use the drugs to the point of dependence or will experience problems related to taking sedatives. Nobody can say for certain how big the problem is, but it is clearly widespread.

Laughing it up—it's a gas

Nitrous oxide (laughing gas), ether and chloroform, the three original anaesthetic gases, were used for their psychological effects well before they were discovered to have anaesthetic properties. During the 19th century, voluntary inhalation of such vapours was a popular recreational pastime among intellectuals and students. Students at Cambridge University held chloroform parties, and Harvard students inhaled ether regularly as a source of pleasure. Nineteenth century descriptions of the effects of these gases sound remarkably like modern reports of LSD 'trips'.

Nitrous oxide (N_2O) was synthesised in 1776 by Sir Humphrey Davy, and soon afterwards Sir Humphrey and interested friends (among them Coleridge, Josiah Wedgwood, and Peter Roget) were using the gas for fun rather than for scientific research.[3] The poet Robert Southey said after one of Davy's nitrous oxide parties that the highest possible heaven must have an atmosphere of N_2O.[4] William James believed the gas had mind-expanding properties.[5]

Nitrous oxide was highly effective and inexpensive, and a number of people—Sir Humphrey included—considered trying to market the gas. Some years later, an American medical student, Gardner Colton, was so successful in his public demonstrations of N_2O that he dropped out of school and went into the laughing gas business. In 1844, Horace Wells, a dentist, observed that a man who tripped and injured himself while under the influence of Colton's N_2O felt no pain. Wells then began to use nitrous oxide on his patients during dental procedures, and the use of N_2O as an anaesthetic spread rather rapidly.[3]

Recreational use of nitrous oxide still exists, although on a smaller scale than in the 1800s. Such use has been reported in many parts of the United States and Canada. Often a professional with access to the anaesthetic gas will bring a supply of N_2O to a party; restaurant workers have been known to inhale the nitrous oxide used to make whipped cream.

The reinforcing properties of anaesthetic gases are not limited to humans. A recent study showed that squirrel monkeys will press a key to self-administer N_2O, but will not continue the behaviour if N_2O is not given. Monkeys will also self-administer ether and chloroform.[4]

Chloroform was discovered in 1831, and its recreational use, at least in the United States, began as soon as the drug was known. Ether, under the trade name *Anodyn*, was marketed in the mid-1900s as a painkiller, but people soon discovered its euphoriant properties. Ether drinking became common in Europe in the later 19th century. As with N_2O, ether drinking was not confined to the poorer classes: 'persons of education and refinement' were among the patients of one inebriologist. In parts of Europe, ether mixes were used by both sexes, young and old alike.[3]

Something to sniff at

Nitrous oxide, ether, and, to a much lesser extent, chloroform are still used for purposes of intoxication. But the modern use of inhalants centres mainly on the volatile solvents such as gasoline and cleaning fluid that are commonly used in industry and commerce. The glue used for making model aeroplanes is the most widely misused of these volatile substances. Contact cements, paint and varnish thinners, lighter fluid, nail polish removers, toluene, benzene, and aerosol propellants round out the list of commercial substances inhaled for their subjective effects.

Generally, 'glue sniffers' squeeze anywhere from one-third to five tubes of glue or cement into a paper or plastic bag. The edges of the bag are then placed around the mouth (and sometimes the nose) and the fumes are inhaled into the lungs. Sniffers of gasoline and other volatile liquids usually inhale the fumes from a rag saturated with the substance. It is either placed in the mouth, over the mouth and nose, or into a bag and sniffed like glue. Direct inhalation—straight from the bottle or can—is also common.

Users of aerosols generally inhale the spray through a rag or filter, which traps the particulate matter while letting the propellant pass. The aerosol can may also be held upside down:

theoretically, only the propellant escapes in this position. The aerosol may also be sprayed into a plastic or paper bag, as with glue, and the propellant gas sniffed from the bag. But some impatient or totally ignorant sniffers even spray the entire contents of the can—propellant and particulates—directly into their mouths, often with fatal results as the particulate matter wreaks havoc with the respiratory system.[4]

What it does to the sniffer

The materials used in sniffing all contain substances that produce complex, but mostly depressant, effects on the central nervous system. The effects of these volatile or gaseous inhalants often include confusion, dizziness and inco-ordination, as well as delusions and visual and auditory hallucinations. Although the general effect is an intoxication similar to alcoholic drunkenness, in some cases the effects resemble those of an hallucinogenic 'trip'. This clearly shows that the inhalants have at least some actions that are distinct from those of alcohol.[4]

Even during their first sniffing experience, users generally have a number of typical reactions, including giddiness, impaired judgement, slurred speech and euphoria. Other effects include numbness, space and colour distortions, sensations of blankness, and feelings of omnipotence and recklessness. Many of the sensations accompanying a sniffing 'high', such as dizziness, lightheadedness and freedom from inhibition, seem similar to those of alcohol intoxication. However, according to sniffers, the feeling of euphoria and omnipotence are much more pronounced with inhalants than with alcohol.

Eeny meeny miney mo, catch a noseful... and here we go!

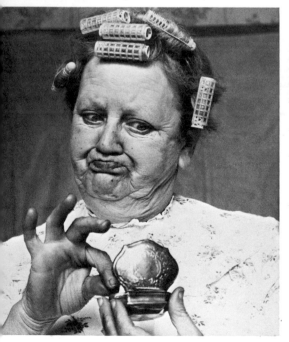
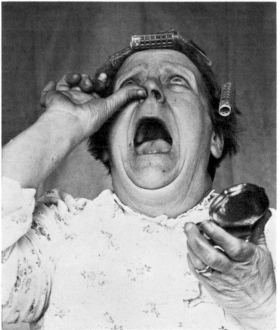

An easy high

The rapid onset of the short-lived intoxication and the relative freedom from unpleasant after-effects make the use of inhalants attractive to teenagers and younger children who want an 'easy high'. This factor also contributed to the popularity of the anaesthetic gases. The effects of N_2O set in within 30 seconds inhalation and last for a short 2–3 minutes. Provided the gas is used with adequate amounts of oxygen, there are minimal adverse effects, with headache being the primary complaint. The same is usually true of ether and chloroform: there is a short, quick high with virtually no hangover.

With most of the inhalants used today, the immediate effects—slurred speech, inco-ordination, euphoria, etc.—begin with the onset of sniffing and last for 15–45 minutes after sniffing ceases. The high can be maintained indefinitely by intermittent sniffing over a long period of time. After the euphoric effects wear off, the user may experience one or two hours of depressant effects, such as drowsiness and stupor; when these sensations wear off, the sniffer returns to his normal state.

Solvent sniffing is frequently practised by groups of young boys. When in group situations, euphoric sniffers often engage in horseplay and sometimes in homosexual activities.

The dangers of sniffing

The possible side effects of solvent sniffing are many and varied. While most of the unpleasant symptoms are not very serious and seem to be reversible, there is no certainty that serious toxicity will not develop. Total or partial amnesia may occur during the period of intoxication. During use and afterwards, the sniffer may experience coughing, irritation of the nose and eyes, nausea, vomiting, diarrhoea, chest, muscle and joint pains, double vision, and extrasensitivity to light. Severe loss of appetite may also develop in frequent sniffers.

Long-term damaging effects of the volatile solvents vary with the specific substance used. Benzene for instance is highly toxic, producing anaemia and damage to the heart, liver, and adrenal glands. Chloroform can cause changes in the rhythm of the heart; even when used by trained medical personnel it can cause rapid fatalities as a result of such effects. Some of the propellants used in aerosols can also alter heart rhythms. Chloroform may also produce damage to the liver. Gasoline inhalation has been known to result in pulmonary bleeding, irritation of the bronchial tubes, anaemia, and cranial nerve paralysis. After long-term low-level exposure in industrial situations, there can be paralysis of peripheral nerves. Lead poisoning from leaded petrol can occur with chronic exposure.

Deaths related to glue and solvent sniffing can come about in one of several ways. The method of solvent inhalation drastically reduces oxygen supply and anoxic damage to the brain may occur. Intoxication may cause abnormal behaviour that leads to accidental injury. Or the solvent may cause acute damage to some organ of the body, such as the heart or liver. A change in heart rhythm is probably the most common cause of casualty associated with solvents, with asphyxiation a close second. Frequently a sniffer will lose consciousness before removing the plastic bag from around his mouth and nose and, if the bag does not fall off of its own accord, will suffocate.

Other solvent-related deaths can result from the sniffer acting out his glue-induced fantasies. Feelings of omnipotence and recklessness may lead to fights, reckless driving, and other dangerous behaviour. Some sniffers experience the delusion of being able to fly, and this had led to inadvertent suicides when sniffers have jumped off roofs or out of windows.[4,5]

In most parts of the world, glue and solvent sniffing is considered a low-class habit, possibly because it is indulged in primarily by young boys in their early teens who tend to come from poor backgrounds. The inhalants are attractive to this particular group of people for a number of reasons. They are readily available—virtually every household has some solvent or aerosol in its cupboards. They are cheap, and easier to steal than drugs or alcohol.

Sniffing is often practised by groups of young people—even in public places.

Although in some areas minors may not buy model aeroplane glue, most inhalants are fully legal. The containers are usually small enough to fit in a pocket, and no complex paraphernalia is needed. Inhalants work quickly, wear off quickly, and, provided there are no cardiac effects or accidents, cause little or no serious hangover.

How many sniffers?

The newspapers of the early 1960s reported many deaths caused by inhalant abuse. However, a bulletin issued by the National Clearinghouse for Poison Control Centers in 1964 claimed that there were actually only nine deaths attributable to glue sniffing. They were apparently reported many times each.[3]

Surveys taken in the United States near the end of the decade (1967–69) indicated that five per cent (about 150,000 annually) of American high school graduates had tried glue at least once. But the use of inhalants now occurs primarily among junior high school students (aged 12–14) and tends to end soon after it begins: 70 per cent of high school students and 75 per cent of junior high students stop after one or two experiences.

A later survey—in 1973—showed that, if use of inhalants was not actually disappearing, at least it was not tremendously popular. Two per cent of the adult American population and six per cent of the youth aged 12–17 had experimented with inhalants. By 1977, the figures had crept up: nine per cent of young people reported some experience with inhalants. Most of the adults, and two thirds of the youth, however, indicated that their last experience with inhalants had been more than a year previously. Only 0·7 per cent of young people had sniffed in the month before the survey. Of those who had never tried inhalants, hardly anybody could be found who definitely wanted to.

Can sniffing be prevented?

In the United States during the 1960s, hundreds of young people were arrested for sniffing glue. Some were even placed in detention homes. Glue sniffing was not illegal at the time, however: children were being arraigned on charges of drunkenness and delinquency for doing things that for an adult would have been perfectly legal. In an attempt to rectify this apparent unfairness, anti-glue laws were passed by many communities.

These laws restricted the use of model aeroplane glue and in some cases prohibited its sale to unaccompanied minors. This can be viewed as a positive step in controlling a drug problem, but as with much other anti-drug regulation, restrictions on glue do not reach the heart of the matter.

Simply reducing the availability of intoxicating solvents by prohibiting their sale does not eliminate the other factors that contribute to drug use. The glue sniffers, both in the United States and in other countries, are young—many as young as seven or eight years old—with an average age of only 14 years. They are commonly from problem homes, in which the parents are frequently heavy drinkers and the father often absent. They have high rates of truancy and delinquent behaviour, and tend to have poor school adjustment and scholastic records.

Many juvenile sniffers are, clearly, children attempting to escape from a troubled reality. Many educators, drug abuse experts, and politicians believe that elementary school health and safety programmes and early diagnosis and correction of unhealthy family or school situations would be an effective way of dealing with the problem of inhalant abuse. Unfortunately, it is far from certain that even our best intentioned efforts to help these young people can make any significant difference to their feelings or behaviour.

6 The chemistry of mysticism

Consciousness expansion, the search for what Dr Sidney Cohen has so aptly termed 'The Beyond Within', is as ancient as man, yet as contemporary as the bewildering alphabet soup of psychoactive substances that flows from the laboratories of modern organic chemistry. LSD, DMT, STP, MDA, TCP, PSP are among the most modern; peyote, 'fly agaric', psilocybin among the more ancient. The total number of these remarkable substances must now be in the thousands, but most are merely chemical curiosities, synthesised symbols of the chemist's ingenuity. A few are sources of profound alarm because of their meteoric rise to popularity and their terrifying capacity to distort our accustomed reality.[1]

The *soma* described in the writings of ancient India (probably *Amanita muscaria*, the 'fly agaric' toadstool) was reputed to 'make one like God'. Psilocybe, 'the divine mushroom' also called 'God's flesh', was held in no less religious esteem by the peoples of Central America long before the rise of Aztec civilisation. Peyote, the mid-altering cactus of the American southwest, remains central to the ritual of the Native American Church, spiritual home of a quarter million American Indians.

Distortion of reality

If these drugs have been part of the sacred, they have also been part of the profane. The many names under which they have been classified convey some of our ambivalence. 'Hallucinogens'—inducers of hallucinations—is probably the most common. It is not quite accurate, however, since few of these drugs produce true hallucination. They do distort reality. Sometimes they have been termed 'psychotomimetic'—capable of mimicking such severe mental illness as schizophrenia. Again, the term is less than apt, since the psychic states produced are usually, though not always, readily distinguished from naturally occurring schizophrenia.

'Psychedelic', the word coined by Dr Humphrey Osmond, emphasises the 'mind-manifesting', 'mind-expanding' proper-

'Another reality'—
or a web of
distortion?

ties of these drugs which were to be celebrated in the 'psychedelic revolution' of the 1960s. Finally, the term 'psycholytic', stressing the ability of some of these drugs to 'dissolve' the psyche, or at least the patient's psychotherapeutic resistance, has sometimes been used. It at least captures the initial optimism that surrounded the introduction of such drugs as LSD and psilocybin as aids to psychotherapy in the 1950s and 1960s.[1]

LSD lysergic acid diethylamide

LSD was originally synthesised in 1938 by two Swiss chemists. But it was not until five years later that one of its co-discoverers, Dr Albert Hofmann, became aware of its profound mind-altering properties. One spring afternoon in 1943, Dr Hofmann became afflicted with great restlessness and dizziness followed by a mild delirium in which he experienced 'fantastic visions of extraordinary vividness accompanied by a kaleidoscopic play of intense colouration'. To verify his suspicions that these bizarre symptoms had been produced by inadvertently ingesting LSD, Hofmann took another 'small' dose—0.25mg of the substance.

The effects this time were even more dramatic. They included not only the visual changes he had noted earlier, but also the fact that 'sounds were transposed into visual sensations so that from each tone or noise a comparable coloured picture was evoked changing in form and colour kaleidoscopically'.[1]

In reality, Hofmann's 'small' dose of LSD was two and a half times that normally required (100 micrograms) for a major LSD 'trip', and over ten times the amount leading to definite psychological effects in most people (20 micrograms). Hofmann had by serendipity discovered the most powerful hallucinogen now known. Dosages are measured in micrograms—millionths of a gram.[1,2] A kilogram would be enough to provide a full scale LSD experience for the total combined populations of London and New York City!

What happens on a trip
Few drugs have so captured the interest and imagination of psychopharmacologists as LSD, and few have been more carefully studied in both animal and human experimentation. Over 2,000 research papers document what is known.

Physiologically, the effects of LSD are usually undramatic. The most obvious sign of ingestion is an enlargement of the pupils. Blood pressure, heart rate and body temperature may increase slightly. Occasionally nausea, chills, flushing and shakiness occur.

But the psychological effects of LSD are as exciting as the physiological effects are dull. Their onset may take anywhere from twenty minutes to two hours. Vision is far more intense and colourful than normal, leading some users to speak of 'seeing for the first time'. Objects may shimmer and undulate as though reflected in 'fun house' mirrors. Sounds are often seen, colours may be heard, sounds such as music smelled—a crossing over of sensory perception called 'synaesthesia'. Hearing, taste, smell and touch are all enhanced and the subjectively slowed sense of time may make the experience seem to go on indefinitely.[2]

A sense of ecstatic detachment, of euphoria, and of loss of one's ego often occur. The user frequently sees enormous symbolic significance in ordinary objects and events. In some, LSD use leads to a profound mystical sense of contact with God or the Infinite.

As with other mind-altering drugs, the effects of LSD are dependent on the user's expectations ('set') and the circumstances ('setting') under which he or she takes the drug. In the laboratory or other supportive setting, using known doses of pure drug with individuals free of major psychological problems, there are likely to be fewer problems than under street conditions. Since LSD heightens the user's suggestibility, he or she is much more likely to have a 'bad trip' if unprepared for the experience, psychologically upset, or anxious.

A 'trip' can let you see God—or it can be an endless nightmare.

Under those circumstances, the effects are far more likely to be terrifying. They may lead the user to believe he or she is 'going crazy' or is about to die. The time distortions may add to the panic by making the experience seem to go on forever. The user may become grandiose about his abilities or become very suspicious; either may lead to irrational behaviour, especially when the usual ego controls are not operating properly.

Counting the costs

Those seeking escape, or ecstasy, will find a way to lose themselves.

An experience as dramatic in its psychological impact as LSD is can certainly be disruptive, particularly in those who are psychologically vulnerable. Although it is hard to know how frequently serious adverse reactions occur compared to the total number of uses of LSD, acute or even chronic psychotic reactions can occur.[2,3]

In one five-year follow-up study of 247 LSD users who had used the drug mostly under medical circumstances, few adverse long-lasting effects were found.[3] However, one problem in studying chronic street users is distinguishing possible personality differences which existed prior to use from those which may be the result of drug use. Chronic users of LSD are also likely to be users of other drugs, making it difficult to distinguish the effects due to each of the various drugs.

Despite the concern about LSD use potentially leading to brain damage or other permanent psychological change, there is little in the research literature suggesting that such effects typically occur or are due to LSD when they do occur. For a time, some researchers believed that chromosomes—the carriers of the genetic heritage—could be damaged by LSD use. More careful research with pure LSD, comparing matched samples of subjects with others who had not received the drug, showed no evidence of this. The research on street users who showed chromosomal irregularities is now thought to have failed to consider such factors as the use of other drugs, higher rates of viral illness that go with a drug-oriented life style, and other aspects of the LSD user's behaviour which may have affected chromosomes.[3]

LSD and psychotherapy

A drug like LSD was bound to interest psychiatrists seeking new ways to understand their patients and better ways to treat them. After World War II, when the properties of LSD became better known, some psychiatrists took it themselves so that they might better understand their patients' mental illness. They also began using the drug as a way of accelerating psychotherapy or gaining psychological access to patients they could not otherwise reach.

The first report of the usefulness of the drug with chronically withdrawn, seriously ill mental patients was published in 1950. It was soon followed by other equally favourable reports on LSD's psychiatric usefulness. LSD was also used with alcoholics and drug addicts, again with initially promising results.[1,3]

Although these earlier reports were mostly favourable, longer term and more careful follow-up studies proved less so. Unfortunately, the marked rise in LSD abuse (see below) and the complex legal restrictions that resulted sharply curtailed clinical use. Even now, over a quarter century later, the question of just how therapeutically valuable LSD is—that is, whether it works, with whom and under what circumstances—is still not entirely clear.

LSD's therapeutic use with dying patients, an application favoured by several American groups, was one of the most innovative clinical uses. The purpose of such treatment was to give the patient, through the LSD experience, a sense that death is not meaningless, but is part of a meaningful larger pattern.

Coming to terms with our own death—life's final challenge. Some doctors believe that L.S.D. can help dying patients make their final peace.

The 'psychedelic revolution'

Until the 1960s, the self-administration of LSD was largely restricted to a small number of intellectuals intrigued by the accounts of its mystical potential and possible value in creativity. According to Dr Richard Blum, an American sociologist who studied some of these early users, their motivation for use was generally quite serious and emphasised longer range philosophical, ethical, and aesthetic objectives, rather than the immediate effects of the LSD experience itself.

Probably the single most influential force in popularising the use of LSD and the so-called 'psychedelic revolution' was Dr Timothy Leary, a young psychologist at Harvard University

59

who became interested in psychedelic substances in about 1960. His research was originally cautious and restrained. But with his own mounting enthusiasm, he and others in his circle used and gave psilocybin to students and to other people more and more indiscriminately.

The resulting adverse publicity forced Leary to leave Harvard. He eventually became a colourfully outspoken advocate of the free use of psychedelic substances after forming his anti-establishment League for Spiritual Discovery. He and others became convinced that LSD experience was the key to a social revolution that could humanise society, eliminate war and effectively eradicate many, if not most, of mankind's social ills.[3]

The mind-benders today

As the use of LSD became more widespread and less discriminating, reports of seriously adverse consequences of use became everyday news. Increasing use, even by young adolescents, led to increasing legal restrictions on 'acid' and wide publicity of the possible dangers of its illicit use. Although there is some continuing use of hallucinogens, the use of LSD probably peaked in the late 1960s in the United States. After a slow decline, it appears to have stabilised at a low level.

In a 1977 government-sponsored national survey in the United States, about 5 per cent of young people (aged 12–17) admitted to having used an hallucinogen at some time in their lives, but only 1·6 per cent indicated that the experience was recent. Interestingly, those over 18 had about the same rate of lifetime use (6·1 per cent) but only 0·5 per cent admitted to using an hallucinogen in the previous month. The figures for both young people and adults have remained about the same since these surveys were begun in 1972. However, this division by age tends to obscure the greater experience of the group of young adults between the ages of 18 and 25, where 20 per cent reported having used a hallucinogen at some time in their lives.

Tolerance and physical dependence
Tolerance develops rapidly to the effects of hallucinogens like LSD and mescalin. After a few days of use, the dose required to produce psychological effects is markedly increased. However, there is no detectable withdrawal syndrome when such drugs are stopped. In general, the use of hallucinogens is episodic, and while there are reports that during the heyday of the psychedelic craze there were 'acid heads' who used hallucinogens every day, such regular use is exceedingly rare.

Only 20 per cent of those who have ever used hallucinogens report using them more than 20 times. In this sense, we can say that while there are users and heavy users of hallucinogens, there are no hallucinogen addicts (compulsive users).

Experimentation with hallucinogens is less common and less

60

socially acceptable than the use of alcohol, cigarettes, or marijuana, and less acceptable even than stimulant or sedative use. Those who experiment with the hallucinogens almost without exception first become users of the more socially acceptable psychoactive substances—tobacco, alcohol, and marijuana, and have experimented first with the stimulants, sedatives and tranquillisers.

Getting the grave message early.

'God's flesh'

Peyote, the 'God's flesh' of Mexico and Central America, is a squat cactus (*Lophophora williamsii*) of notably nondescript appearance. But for the fact that its 'buttons' contain the natural hallucinogen mescalin, it would attract little interest.

Mescalin was among the first hallucinogens to be chemically isolated (in 1896, by the German chemist Heffter), and attracted widespread intellectual interest early in this century. Like LSD, it was initially thought to produce a 'model psychosis', an idea later discarded as it became apparent that the state produced differed significantly from mental illness.

Although mescalin belongs to a different chemical class than LSD and psilocybin, both types of hallucinogen seem to exert a similar action in the brain. They both appear to affect the substance *serotonin*. However, the dose of mescalin required to produce such effects is much higher than that of LSD (0·0001gm of LSD as against 0·5gm of mescalin).[2] Since mescalin is rarely available illicitly, its use is almost entirely restricted to the 250,000 Indian members of the Native American Church of North America who regularly consume the bitter, nauseating peyote buttons in which it is contained.

The sacred mushroom

Psilocybin, the active ingredient of the mushroom *Psilocybe mexicana*, is another of the ancient hallucinogens whose colourful ritual use among the cultures of Mexico and Central America is known to date back to at least 1500 BC. It was not until the 1950s, however, that psilocybin was isolated from 'the sacred mushroom'.

The potency of psilocybin is somewhere intermediate between mescalin and LSD. Despite a street mythology that the three drugs have subtly different effects, laboratory studies have found the effects of psilocybin to be very much like those of LSD (assuming appropriate dosage adjustments to take into account the differing potencies).[2] Like mescalin, psilocybin is rare to the point of being non-existent 'on the street'.

Psilocybin was briefly used in conjunction with psychotherapy in the 1950s and 1960s, but there is no evidence that it was any more or less useful for that purpose than LSD.

Angel dust—or the Devil's?

'Angel dust', 'crystal', 'horse tranquilliser', 'rocket fuel'—those are a few of the street names for *phencyclidine*, or PCP, the drug now most rapidly increasing in popularity in North America. In one year, from 1976 to 1977, its use doubled among 12 to 17-year-old Americans and increased by nearly half among 18 to 25-year-olds. So far, there have been only scattered reports of its use elsewhere, but the ease with which PCP can be manufactured and the cohesiveness of the international youth culture virtually guarantee that PCP will soon be a problem everywhere in the developed world.

Phencyclidine is typical of a whole new range of abusable drugs which are likely to be part of the wave of the future. They do not need to be smuggled across international borders because they can be readily manufactured in small clandestine laboratories which are not easily detected. Their profit potential is enormous.

Phencyclidine was developed in 1959 as the first of a new class of anaesthetic agents. Under their influence the patient becomes detached or dissociated from all bodily sensations and feels no pain during surgery—hence the term 'dissociative anaesthetic'. As promising as this new anaesthetic was, it had one unfortunate problem: patients often became very agitated, delusional and irrational while recovering from its anaesthetic effects. Abandoned by physicians, PCP is still occasionally used by veterinarians for immobilising animals, particularly monkeys.

A drug of many masks

As a drug of abuse, phencyclidine had an inauspicious beginning. It made its street debut as the 'peace pill' in San Francisco in the mid-1960s and became an overnight 'failure' because of accidental overdoses with some deaths. PCP was promptly abandoned as a recreational drug of choice by most users. The underground drug went still farther underground and became a drug of many masks, used to dilute or replace other drugs that were more expensive or more difficult to synthesise. Before 1975, only one in 33 street samples found to contain PCP by one West Coast laboratory had actually been sold as PCP. The rest had been misrepresented as exotic or more sought after drugs such as LSD, THC (the psychoactive ingredient in marijuana), mescalin and psilocybin. Some samples even masqueraded as cocaine.

Then drug users learned that PCP, instead of being swallowed, could be smoked or snorted (like snuff). These techniques enable the experienced user to control the dose of the drug and to achieve the desired effect without the dangers of overdose that accompany ingestion. With that important development, PCP use burgeoned.

Phencyclidine in its pure form is a water-soluble crystalline white powder. In street form, it comes in many colours, may be sold as a pill, powder or liquid, and is frequently sprayed on parsley, mint or other leafy material to be smoked as a 'joint'. Because it is still sold under the guise of other drugs and has so many street names, the casual user may not even know that he or she has used PCP.[4]

When sold as a granular powder—'angel dust'—it is usually much purer than in other forms. There may be as little as five per cent drug content when sprayed on material to be smoked.

Angel Dust—a quick ride to madness.

Phencyclidine and its chemical relatives or analogues are difficult to control by law because they can be so easily synthesised. The starting chemicals are in widespread industrial use; the equipment needed is simple; 'recipes' for making the drugs are readily available, and no special skill is required. Apart from the legal hazards, the biggest danger of illicit manufacture is explosion if the materials used are not handled carefully.

What happens when you take 'angel dust'?

This family of drugs exerts a number of actions on the body that are not shared by other drugs. They are therefore generally placed in a distinct category, separate from LSD and psilocybin—and also from cannabis. The most dramatic of PCP's effects so closely mimics acute schizophrenia that psychiatrists have often failed to recognise their origins.

Bizarre behaviour of many types sometimes occurs in response to various delusions and hallucinations (usually of hearing; occasionally of sight). Speech is often 'blocked'—to the outsider it may also appear meaningless. Paranoid thinking is common. In response to imagined threats, or to the police who may intervene because of irrational behaviour, users may react with frightening violence. Because PCP has anaesthetic actions, touch and pain

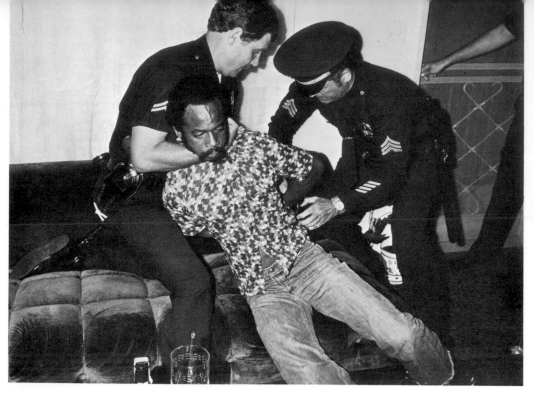

Aggressive behaviour coupled with insensitivity to pain produce violent situations.

sensations are dulled, making the user unusually resistant to outside physical control. The user may severely injure or even kill himself because of an inability to respond to some hazard, or because his perception or thinking is markedly distorted.

The 'body image' of the user is also seriously altered; difficultly in co-ordinating body movements is common. At still higher doses the user may lapse into coma and sometimes die because of the drug's depressant effect on the brain's respiratory centre.[4]

In 1973, in one area of Washington, DC in which PCP use was common, Dr Paul Luisada, a local psychiatrist, noted that 'the admission rate for what appeared to be unusually long, severe, and treatment-resistant initial schizophrenic psychoses suddenly tripled. . . .These patients had all smoked a drug called "angel dust" before becoming psychotic.'

Given these dramatic symptoms, it may seem surprising that phencyclidine was not immediately suspected. But the link between symptoms and cause was elusive. Laboratory tests for PCP were not routine and were unlikely to be performed on patients who did not appear to have typical drug-induced psychoses. Even surveys of emergency rooms, drug crisis centres, and of the general population often missed PCP because it was lumped with other hallucinogens, or because users did not realise they had used it or remember having taken it. The initially bad street reputation of PCP and the obviously unpleasant symptoms that came to attention made it hard to understand why anyone would want to use the drug and once having used it would continue its use.

Why is PCP used?

The early reports on PCP use emphasised the negative effects of the drug, but told only part of the story. Dr Ronald Siegel, a psychologist in Los Angeles, systematically tested and interviewed 310 adult PCP users to learn why they used it.

All agreed that on every occasion of PCP use there were unpleasant, negative aspects to the experience. Positive effects were experienced on only 60 per cent of the occasions the drug was taken, but such feelings were important to the user.[4]

Among the more frequently reported positive PCP effects Siegel's users described are the following: heightened sensitivity to outside stimuli, dissociation, elevation in mood, inebriation, and relaxation. Only one in 12 reported experiencing euphoria.

Negative effects were as common as positive ones: perceptual disturbances, restlessness, disorientation, and anxiety. A quarter to a third of the sample reported such troublesome effects as paranoia, hyperexcitability, irritability and mental confusion. Four out of five reported having problems with their speech.

Drs Michael and Beverly Fauman, studied a sample of 25 chronic PCP users in treatment. While about half reported their initial PCP experience was intensely positive, the rest reported it had been either neutral or mildly unpleasant. Only seven reported that their *typical* PCP experience was positive.

Although most users mention the positive aspects, most also stress that PCP is a hazardous drug and that its effects are not always nor even generally pleasant. Why do they continue? Some clinicians believe that the very unpredictability of the PCP 'drug trip' provides a sense of adventure and excitement. There are apparently many for whom the change from their usual state is welcome, even when the altered state is not more pleasant.

Finally, we know that phencyclidine is unlike hallucinogens such as LSD in that animals will self-administer it as they will such drugs as heroin, morphine, amphetamine, cocaine and alcohol. This indicates that PCP has a more complex or different mode of action in the brain.

Unravelling the mystery

Much remains to be learned about PCP, ranging from the basic neurophysiology to the effects of chronic use. There have been clinical reports that regular phencyclidine users continue to have problems with their speech even after they discontinue the drug. Moreover, it is commonly believed by users themselves that PCP use can cause intellectual deterioration.

Like many other street beliefs about drugs, this has not yet been carefully explored. Since the prevalence of PCP use among young adults in the United States jumped from 9·5 per cent to 14 per cent between 1976 and 1977, the need for more information is becoming urgent.

7 Marijuana—drug for all seasons

Marijuana, grass, pot, dagga, hashish, ganja—these are but a few of the dozens of names for the drug products of the Indian hemp plant, Cannabis sativa. Of all recreational drug use, that of marijuana is the most controversial. Advocates of marijuana use argue that the health hazards are no greater, and possibly less, than those of using alcohol or tobacco, and that therefore its use should be permitted on a similar basis. But most policy-makers are concerned about the unknown risks of adding yet another recreational drug to the two which already exact such a high cost; they believe that we need caution more than consistency.

The ubiquitous hemp plant has been a source of fibre for rope and cloth for centuries. In countries such as India and Nepal, the plant has also been used as a drug for hundreds, perhaps thousands, of years. The traditional users in these societies—and others where the drug has been established for a long time—have been from the poorest, least educated classes.

But in recent years a whole new class of users has developed, first in the prosperous societies of the West and then, by a reverse influence, in the countries from which the drug itself has traditionally come. These new users are likely to be from the middle or upper classes, under twenty-five years old and part of the international 'youth culture'. And, while the number of traditional users has remained stable, the new group has grown explosively.

In the United States, which has been in the vanguard of this new use, an estimated 10 million people had tried cannabis by 1969. By 1977, that number had increased more than fourfold to 43 million, a fifth of the total population. Such countries as Australia, Great Britain, Sweden, the Netherlands and West Germany have had less dramatic but still large increases in use, especially among their students. And, in countries like India, Egypt and Jamaica, the sons and daughters of the elite classes are not patterning their cannabis use on local tradition but on the fashionable use of the drug by young people in other countries. This explosion of cannabis use has aroused worldwide concern and renewed scientific interest in the implications of using this ancient intoxicant.[1]

For a whole generation marijuana is a basic part of 'having a good time'.

Grass, hash and hash-oil

Herbal marijuana or 'grass' is a mixture of crushed leaves, flowers and often twigs of *cannabis sativa*, a plant which now grows throughout the warmer regions of the world although it is thought to have originated in Asia. Its principal psychoactive ingredient, delta-9-tetrahydrocannabinol (THC for short), is most heavily concentrated in the plant's resin. The concentrated dark, tarry resin is called *hashish* and is the usual form in which cannabis is consumed—generally by mixing it with tobacco and smoking it in Europe and the Near East. A still more concentrated form of the drug, hashish oil, can be produced by a percolation process.

Generally, the leafy mixtures contain the smallest amount of THC—usually from one to ten per cent. Hashish contains about ten per cent THC: hashish oil may be as high as 50 to 60 per cent THC. Since the THC contained in cannabis preparations deteriorates, especially when exposed to heat and light, a given sample of marijuana or hashish may vary quite a bit in psychoactivity over a period of time.

Although THC is the most important single cannabis ingredient, others of the plant's one hundred or more chemicals may play some role in modifying the effects of the drug. Only a few of the other components have been studied and their complex interactions are not yet understood.

Marijuana or hashish is usually smoked, but it can be, and sometimes is, eaten. When eaten, it requires from two and a half to three times the amount to produce the same effect as smoking a given quantity. The onset of effect is slower and the effect lasts longer. Marijuana is usually smoked either as a 'joint'—a hand-rolled cigarette—or in pipes ranging from the simple cone-shaped *chillum* used in India, to elaborate water pipes such as the traditional *hookah* of the Middle East or the 'bong' so popular in the United States.

Alleged effects—fact or fiction?

Despite many hundreds of years of use and the accumulated folk wisdom that has resulted, some of the alleged effects of cannabis are paradoxical. Among Indian holy men, for example, cannabis has traditionally been used to 'still the animal spirits'—to reduce libido or sexual drive. Yet among the new breed of users, marijuana has a widespread street reputation as an aphrodisiac. While marijuana has been held by many to lead to a loss of conventional desire to work—the 'amotivational syndrome'—in some countries, like Jamaica, a *ganja* break is taken for much the same purpose as our coffee or tea break in the office or factory.

In India, cannabis has been used as an aid to meditation or clearer thinking, but in Western societies it is believed to be disruptive of memory and to thinking. As we shall see, some of these differences in effect may be explained by the expectations of the user and the setting of use; others may reflect differences produced by the amount and pattern of use (dose-response effects). Nevertheless, much confusion remains. Even for those with scientific training, it is difficult to distinguish fact from fiction.

How high is stoned?

The immediate physiological effects of being 'high' or 'stoned' are undramatic—a reddening of the eyes and an increased heart rate are the most obvious. The subjective experience is much more varied. If you were to smoke a single 'joint' about the size of an ordinary cigarette (containing about 10 milligrams of THC, the main psychoactive ingredient) you would probably be aware of your increased pulse rate, perhaps initially of a vague apprehension and of time appearing 'slowed'—five minutes might feel more like half an hour.

As you continued to smoke you might become quite relaxed—'laid back'. Sensations such as hearing, taste, touch and smell might seem unusually vivid. Something mildly amusing might seem hilarious. You might find yourself having trouble with your memory or concentration, being unable to remember just what point you were making, or even forgetting the beginning of your sentence by the time you got to the end of it.

But you might also find the sensations unpleasant, unnatural, even frightening, or find yourself feeling an irrational suspiciousness of those around you, a fear that in some vaguely undefinable way they were 'out to get you'. With very high doses, or if you are unusually sensitive to the drug, changes such as visual distortions or body image alterations might be frightening enough for you to become very anxious, even panicky, possibly fearful that you were going mad.[2]

Learning the ups and downs
The 'high' which begins within a few minutes of smoking active marijuana (some samples are virtually inert and contain little or no THC) continues for about two or three hours, depending partly on the amount of drug, partly on the individual. To some extent, being high is learned; more experienced users, aware of what to expect, may be better able to perceive the drug's effects (this is sometimes called 'reversed tolerance'), but heavy habitual users also develop a true tolerance to cannabis.[2]

Most experienced users believe they can, if necessary (and if the amount used was not excessive), 'bring themselves down' from their 'high' to meet ordinary work demands or to appear 'normal' to others. Laboratory evidence supports this subjective impression to some extent.[2]

As with other psychoactive drugs, no two 'highs', even for the same person, are likely to be identical. As with alcohol, marijuana may enhance or deepen the mood you are in before using it; your

His and Hers joints—part of togetherness.

depression may increase or, if exhilarated, you may become still more so. Your expectations are also important and these are based partly on your cultural background. In Jamaica, among traditional users, the 'high' sought by most recreational users is neither expected nor experienced. Instead, the drug is used to make demanding labour less burdensome, to lighten the work day.[3]

The question of addiction

It is clear that just as some people enjoy the effects of opiates, alcohol or cocaine, some people enjoy the effects that cannnabis produces. But to what extent do marijuana users become addicted? Do they experience adverse social or medical effects but still find themselves unable to stop? Do they experience withdrawal effects?

These questions are more difficult to answer for cannabis than for the opioids or alcohol. Certainly cannabis is not a powerful reinforcer in laboratory animals. While monkeys and rats will work hard to get an injection of opioids, cocaine or alcohol, they refuse to work to get cannabis unless they have previously learned to work for another more powerful reinforcer.

In western countries where marijuana competes with other recreational drugs such as alcohol, a substantial proportion of young adults have tried marijuana at some time. But only a small proportion of these use it on a continuing basis and, until recently, it was relatively uncommon to find people who use it every day. In recent surveys in the United States, nine per cent of young marijuana users reported daily use.[1] In Moslem and Hindu countries where alcohol is less readily available, everyday heavy use of cannabis, with what appears to be an inability to stop, is not unusual.

A bad connection. Perhaps those who become dependent on cannabis in one culture are those who would be vulnerable to becoming alcoholic in another.

It is possible that where the drug is used daily in high doses, physical dependence does play some small role in perpetuating its use. In an experiment in the United States, subjects who were given oral THC every four hours around the clock did experience some mild withdrawal when the drug was discontinued. However, the withdrawal syndrome is not as unpleasant or distressing as the opioid withdrawal syndrome. Other researchers report that hospitalised subjects smoking several marijuana cigarettes a day for 20–40 days rarely complained specifically about withdrawal when the experiments ended, even though they showed restlessness and disturbed sleep.[2]

Marijuana's effects on performance

Marijuana users often report that their sight, hearing and touch are exquisitely enhanced by cannabis use. But objective measures have been unable to confirm any increased acuity. However, even if the senses are no more objectively acute, it is possible that the user is more aware of them than usual and is therefore more perceptive.

Time perception is altered in a way consistent with the subjective feeling that things 'last longer'. The problems with recent memory, reflected in forgetting what one has just said, have been carefully studied. Scientists now believe the drug interferes with the process of transferring immediate experience to recent memory storage in the brain.[2] Although users often report markedly enhanced appetite, there is no evidence of altered blood sugar levels or other obvious physiological reason for this. It may be that the taste of food is subjectively enhanced by the 'high'.

Performance on various tests and measures depends largely on how familiar the task is, how well it has been previously learned and how complex it is. Generally, the more complex the task, especially if it involves recent memory, and the less well learned it is, the more the ability to perform is diminished by being high.

Marijuana also seems to affect the way in which the two hemispheres of the brain work. The left hemisphere is now believed to be more concerned with reasoning and 'intellectual' problem solving while the right is more concerned with aesthetic, artistic, holistic judgements. Experiments show that, while 'high', performance which is left-hemisphere-dominated is degraded, but right-hemisphere-dominated performance is enhanced.[2]

One of the most important areas of everyday functioning adversely affected by marijuana is driving. While early research suggested that the effects on driving were minimal, more carefully conducted recent research now indicates that marijuana plus driving is as poor a combination as alcohol plus driving.

One especially worrying piece of evidence is that some of the visual problems created by marijuana use may persist for several hours beyond the subjective 'high' feeling. For example, peripheral vision does not recover immediately. While more research is needed, driving while 'stoned' is clearly dangerous. The combination of alcohol and cannabis, which is increasingly common, may be even more dangerous than either alone.

Some other effects
For most users in good health the immediate effects of being 'high' are not serious. The heart rate may increase by as much as 40 to 50 beats a minute, but this is no greater than the increase which occurs during such ordinary exertion as, say, running to catch a bus.[2]

But for some, even occasional use may be serious. American scientists studying the effects of marijuana on chest pain (angina) in heart patients found that it caused pain more quickly and following less effort than did tobacco cigarettes. Others who should probably not experiment with marijuana are those who have had serious emotional problems: a study of a small group of recovered patients who had had schizophrenia found that the illness consistently recurred following cannabis use. Among college students, it has been found that those who worry more about their health and who feel less in control of their lives are more likely to find marijuana use frightening and unpleasant than those who do not.

Marijuana's metabolites (the products of its physiological transformation in the body) remain in the body fat for some days after each use. Some scientists have speculated on the possibility that it may have unexpectedly dangerous effects on the body by interfering with the building blocks of cell replacement. There is some animal evidence that cannabis can affect cell metabolism but there is as yet no indication that these changes are injurious. Just what the implications of the persistence of cannabis in body fat are is not yet known.

Effects of chronic use

Most scientists agree that infrequent use of small quantities of typical marijuana rarely leads to serious medical problems in healthy adults. But this should not lull us into believing that cannabis is 'safe'. Despite the many millions who have used the drug and the many hundreds of years that the drug has been used, not a great deal is known about its chronic effects. Still less is known about the effects of its use by children and adolescents who are in the vanguard of the new breed of cannabis users.

So little is known partly because there are formidable problems in studying chronic use. In most countries with a long history of use, users and non-users alike are not very long-lived, especially if they are poor (as is the typical user). The levels of work performance required may be much lower than in modern industrial societies and so may be less sensitive to the effects of the drug. Few of the countries involved are rich enough to afford large scale health surveys of the type that may be required to explore marijuana health risks adequately. Newer patterns of use in more developed countries are very recent and, because they involve the healthiest segment of the population, are unlikely so far to have had easily detectable large-scale health consequences.

Several major studies (in Jamaica, Costa Rica and Greece) have carefully matched chronic user groups with non-users of similar background. These have found few important differences between the two groups.[3, 5] Although the hashish smokers in Greece were more often diagnosed as having 'anti-social' personality characteristics, this seemed to be more a cause of their hashish use rather than a consequence of it.[5]

Although these three recent scientific research projects have often been cited by cannabis advocates as indicating that the drug is 'safe', such a conclusion is both premature and ignores other research findings. The total number of user-nonuser pairs in all three projects—117—was too small to detect rarer consequences of use. For example, had similarly sized samples of cigarette smokers in middle life been studied, it is unlikely that some of the most serious consequences of tobacco smoking— lung cancer, heart disease and emphysema—would have been detected. And the psychological tests that were used, because of the low performance of both user and nonuser groups, may have been insensitive to differences between the groups.

Large-scale studies of American college student populations at such universities as the University of California at Berkeley have found no evidence that regular marijuana users are less successful academically than are non-users. However, the low levels of use involved (compared to chronic use in other countries), the possibility that those whose performance had been impaired may have dropped out before the study and the generally high levels of motivation in this population all make it less likely that differences would have been found.

Sources of concern

Although the evidence to date is far from clear cut, several important problem areas related to cannabis use have emerged from recent research.

Since marijuana and hashish are usually smoked, interference with lung function might be expected. As early as the Indian Hemp Drugs Commission Report of 1894, the possibility that cannabis could cause bronchitis was raised. More recently, when hashish-using American soldiers stationed in Europe were studied, they frequently complained of bronchitis. When cells from their air passages were examined under the microscope, changes like those of much older, heavy cigarette smokers were discovered.

The Leuchtenbergers, a Swiss husband–wife research team, have reported that human lung tissue exposed to cannabis smoke in the test tube showed more serious cell alterations than occurred when similar tissue samples were exposed to standard tobacco smoke. The changes found were like those in cancer cells. When extracts of cannabis smoke are placed on the skin of test animals, tumours are produced similar to those produced by tobacco tar.[4]

Taking all the evidence into account, it seems likely that the heavy use of marijuana will eventually be shown to be hazardous to health in a way similar to that of cigarettes. Since many use both, the combined risk may be more serious than that of either alone.

The immune response
The single most important factor that keeps us well—more important than lack of exposure to disease or even good sanitation—is the body's immune responses, its inherent ability to fight off disease. We know that so-called 'T-cell immunity' is impaired in cancer patients and gradually becomes less effective as we become elderly.

At present, there is much scientific controversy over whether chronic marijuana use suppresses the immune response. Some scientists have found what they interpret as reductions in this vital response; but others have not obtained the same findings. Several animal studies using high, but still humanly relevant, doses of marijuana or of THC have found that the animal's immunity was reduced. One way this question may ultimately be settled is to study a group of users who show 'test-tube' evidence of impaired immunity over a period of time to see if they are in practice more disease-susceptible than non-users.[1,4]

Marijuana and Reproduction

Several years ago, it was suggested that cannabis use might damage chromosomes—the essential material through which our genetic heritage is transmitted to future generations. Subsequent genetic studies found no evidence of chromosome changes related to use. There is at present no really convincing indication that significant genetic changes result from using cannabis.

The evidence that marijuana can produce a practically significant reduction in the male hormone testosterone is also questionable: such reductions, when found, have not been to abnormally low levels, and not all researchers have found them, even in long-term chronic users.

There have also been reports of reductions in the number of sperm and isolated clinical reports of impaired sexual performance in men related to heavy cannabis use. However, long-term user studies in Jamaica, Greece and Costa Rica found no evidence that family size was reduced in users. These findings may be of significance primarily for those with already impaired fertility or hormonal problems.

The female response

Women make up an increasing proportion of cannabis users, but little work has been done on specifically female responses to the drug. Animal research has not produced evidence that in the usual quantities the drug reduces fertility or causes abnormal births (although at very high levels—nor humanly relevant—it does).

On the other hand, a comparison of sexual hormone levels in 30 women who had used cannabis three or more times a week for six months or more with a group of non-using women found evidence that fertility might be impaired in users. Other factors may have affected these findings, but users were more likely to have menstrual cycles in which an egg did not ripen or in which the period of fertility was foreshortened.

'The milk of human kindness'—but who knows what the baby is taking in along with mother's milk?

Marijuana and the brain

In 1971, a British team reported that ten young male cannabis users exhibited brain shrinkage—similar to that in advanced old age—after from three to eleven years of using the drug. The potential importance of such a finding led to several more carefully controlled pieces of research, none of which found any evidence of the type of brain atrophy originally reported. Significant brain damage can, of course, occur without it becoming anatomically obvious. But none of the research that has been done to date has found evidence of persistently impaired psychological functioning as a concomitant of cannabis use.

One scientist used deeply implanted electrodes in the brains of monkeys, which were given cannabis over a long period. He reported changes in brain electrical activity and microscopic cellular changes in the brains. While such experiments show that subtle changes in brain anatomy or function may occur, the practical implications, if any, of such findings are not at present known. Others have found temporary brain wave changes related to being 'high', but no evidence of lasting abnormality.[2]

Does marijuana lead to other drugs?

Observers in the United States and Great Britain frequently noted that most heroin addicts had previously used marijuana. Some people believed that in some way marijuana use led to opiate addiction. If this means that, in some pharmacological or physiological sense, cannabis use 'causes' later heroin use, the statement is false. Most cannabis users do not use heroin or other stronger drugs. But, in the new class of users, those who use more heavily are better described as polydrug users, and often use many different drugs such as cocaine and the hallucinogens.

Just why this is so is not entirely clear, but whatever the reasons there is a statistical association between marijuana use and that of other drugs only in the sense that the heavier marijuana user is considerably more likely to have experimented with other licit *and* illicit mind-altering drugs than is the lighter user who is, in turn, more likely to have done so than someone who does not use cannabis at all.

Psychological hazards

She knows how to roll a good joint—but maybe more essential learning is going up in smoke.

Many kinds of psychological problems—from a loss of conventional motivation to serious mental illness—have been attributed to cannabis use. In the extreme case of someone who is almost continuously heavily intoxicated, there is little question that 'the drug' interferes with other activity. But when we turn to the user who uses heavily although not constantly the question is harder.

Despite the widespread belief in countries of traditional use that motivation is seriously affected, none of the three modern studies in Jamaica, Greece or Costa Rica found evidence of this. Experimental studies of users in controlled laboratory situations have not found diminished productivity overall although at the height of intoxication work levels were sometimes reduced.[1,2]

But when one turns to the question of the impact of heavy marijuana use on children and teenagers there is a unanimity of professional opinion regarding the *undesirability* of use even though there is little research evidence that can be cited.

Two kinds of problems are involved. Since childhood and adolescence are periods of rapid growth and skill acquisition, there is good reason to be concerned that chronic intoxication, whether with marijuana or other drugs, may interfere physiologically or psychologically with those processes. A second concern is based on a kind of 'behavioural toxicity' related to marijuana use—users are more likely to be deviant in other ways, such as truancy, alcohol use and delinquency, and will exert 'peer pressure' on new recruits to conform to deviant patterns.

Probably the most common adverse psychological reaction in the inexperienced user or inadvertent over-user is panic or acute anxiety that the changed thinking produced by the drug will persist. This abates as the drug wears off.

The most serious psychological reaction attributed to cannabis is the *cannabis psychosis*, an illness with some symptoms like those of schizophrenia, often accompanied by violent behaviour. Such serious reactions have been reported in India and other countries of traditional use, but appear to be uncommon in Europe and North America. Because this label is used so freely in some countries, it is often difficult to know whether the condition is the result of cannabis use alone or of earlier mental illness which may be aggravated by the use of the drug. Recent studies in the United States suggest that those with histories of mental illness may be more vulnerable to adverse effects.

Marijuana, criminality and aggression

Anti-marijuana propaganda of the 1920s and 1930s often included lurid anecdotes of serious crimes and violence allegedly resulting from the use of marijuana.

But there is no convincing objective evidence that cannabis use as such leads to crime (aside from the crime of possessing the drug itself). Most laboratory studies have found that, while 'high', aggression is actually decreased (unlike alcohol intoxication which often increases violent behaviour), and the weight of evidence seems to be that cannabis does not lead to violence.[1,2]

Is cannabis an aphrodisiac?

Throughout recorded history, and probably long before, a succession of substances—from oysters to truffles—have been thought to be aphrodisiac. Thinking has sometimes made then so. Many drugs—alcohol is a good example—can serve to reduce inhibitions, making sexual behaviour more likely. But there is serious doubt whether any can create desire where it is absent.

Although the amount of evidence concerning marijuana's effect on sexuality is modest—it is a difficult research area—limited work has been done. Erich Goode, an American sociologist, interviewed over 200 marijuana-using men and women in their twenties, specifically asking them about the drug's sexual effects on them.

More than a third said it had no effect; a few said it had a negative effect. Some felt it depended on their mood or on their sexual partner. But nearly half felt that marijuana definitely increased their sexual desire. And the vast majority—over two thirds—said that it increased their sexual pleasure. One explanation may be that the drug induces a greater sensitivity to nuances of sensation—whether visual, olfactory or sexual.

Pharmacologically, marijuana, like alcohol, may reduce sexual inhibitions; but, like alcohol, the effect may backfire. Too much may result in a loss of interest in sex or an inability to perform.

Passion—Marijuana can't create it, but it can heighten sexual pleasure.

Medical uses

The earliest known pharmacopoeia, the *Pen Ts'oo China*, a Chinese list of remedies compiled nearly 20 centuries ago, recommended cannabis as an anaesthetic in surgery. Cannabis has been used in the folk medicine of many lands for treating such varied ills as cholera, malaria, diarrhoea, seizures (fits), loss of appetite, loss of memory, cough, rheumatism, insomnia and toothache.

It was introduced into Western medicine in 1839 by W. B. O'Shaughnessy, a British physician then serving in India. Cannabis continued to be used as a sedative, as a treatment for neuralgia, menstrual pain and migraine headaches well into the twentieth century, when it was gradually displaced by other more stable synthetic drugs.

One of the 'fringe benefits' of recent marijuana research has been a renewed medical interest in this ancient remedy. Recently cannabis or its active ingredient THC have been tried for such diverse purposes as treating alcoholics, controlling seizures and relieving pain, all with equivocal results. However, a promising new use was discovered when young cancer patients found that smoking marijuana seemed to prevent the previously uncontrollable nausea and vomiting commonly produced by powerful anti-cancer medications. Research is still going on, but it now appears likely that this will become an acceptable medical use.[1]

A second use which shows promise is reducing the pressure within the eye of the glaucoma patient—a pressure which, if not relieved, ultimately causes blindness. While systematically studying the effects of known doses of marijuana on young male volunteers, scientists found that marijuana reduced eye pressure. They reasoned that if this happened in normal people, perhaps it would also happen in glaucoma victims. It does. While we do not yet know how persistently effective the drug will be, its freedom from some of the serious side effects of other drugs may make it a valuable medicine.

Another discovery in these normal volunteers may also prove to be enduringly useful. Physiologists found that marijuana, while a lung irritant, also consistantly increased the size of the air passages. The researchers therefore tried marijuana as well as aerosol THC in treating asthmatics: both relieved the symptoms. There are other effective drugs for this same purpose, but the mode of action of THC is different. It may thus be useful in cases where other drugs are ineffective.

The drugs that ultimately result from cannabis research may bear only slight resemblance to the natural material. Through modern organic chemistry it is possible to modify the molecules of a drug substance in such a way that the desired therapeutic qualities are preserved and undesirable side effects are minimised or eliminated. THC may thus be modified so that it does not produce a high, but continues to reduce nausea, eye pressure or the asthmatic's bronchial spasms.

Trends for the future

The marked increase in cannabis use among the youth of Europe and North America may well be on its way to becoming an enduring pattern of recreational drug use. When it originally began in countries like Canada and the United States in the 1960s, marijuana use had a distinctly symbolic 'counter-culture' aspect. It was typically weak and used infrequently by a minority even of young people.

But what was once a minority behaviour has now become a majority phenomenon—three out of five Americans aged 18 to 25 had used cannabis by 1977. That use has now become even heavier, more habitual and begins earlier in life. Although equally detailed trend data are not available for other countries of Europe and North America, there is good reason for believing use is steadily increasing elsewhere as well.

'Now let's get the atmosphere right...'

Although more than 3,000 research papers have been published on cannabis since 1964, many important questions remain unanswered. Much less is known about the health hazards of chronic use than about the dangers of alcohol and tobacco. And it is likely that it will take many millions of man-years of widespread use and large-scale studies to detect the subtler, less common risks.

Use by the very young of a drug whose use can be so easily concealed poses special problems which its advocates have often chosen to ignore. For example, it is unlikely that a scheme can be devised which could successfully restrict use to adults any more than this has been possible with cigarettes. Unlike drunkenness with its slurred speech, incoordination and telltale breath, being high is more easily disguised. In the era of the automobile, a method of determining whether someone is driving while high is as essential as blood alcohol tests, but it is much more difficult to devise.

If cannabis use continues to expand at its present rate, it may be necessary to rethink our approach to regulation despite the hazards. At present, the criminal penalties fall capriciously on a very small proportion of users and appear to have, at best, a tiny deterrent value on the population as a whole. In the meantime, illicit traffickers reap huge profits while the burdens of any adverse effects fall on the shoulders of users and non-users alike. Yet there is no way of altogether anticipating the social hazards that a new drug coming into widespread use will pose. A reappraisal of policy will require our best judgement and ingenuity.

8 Tobacco — the devil's weed

As far as we can tell, tobacco was not known to Europeans or Asians until the discovery of the New World. On his arrival in the West Indies, Indians greeted Columbus with dried leaves of a native plant. To them, the leaves were precious and the gift was a token of esteem. Columbus and his crew threw the leaves overboard. But on the island of Cuba the Spaniards found Indians rolling these leaves into tubes, setting fire to them, and inhaling the smoke. Rodrigo de Jerez, a member of the landing party, became the first European smoker and brought the practice back to Spain. By the beginning of the 17th century, Europeans knew tobacco as a medical herb. Pipe smoking had become equally well known as a habit indulged in by princes and commoners, men, women and children.[1]

No power to stop puffers

Those who did not enjoy smoking regarded the habit as offensive. The diversity and intensity of their efforts to prevent it are remarkable for their universal failure.

King James I of England was probably the first sovereign to denounce smoking—in 1604—as an abominable social practice. But despite royal opposition and the exorbitant price of tobacco (worth its weight in silver), Englishmen continued to smoke.

Rulers in other parts of the world made even more vigorous efforts to control tobacco during the 17th century. The first Romanoff czars instituted severe criminal penalties—including public whipping and exile to Siberia—for its possession, use or sale. However, when Peter the Great came to power in 1689, smoking became an accepted practice. In Japan, too, after initial attempts to prohibit its use, tobacco smoking finally became an integral part of social ritual.

The first cigarettes

For its first 250 years in the Old World, tobacco was smoked in pipes and cigars, sniffed as snuff, and chewed. The cigarette, which is the most destructive form of tobacco use, did not make its appearance until the mid-19th century. The invention of a

*Tobacco—used for
centuries in the New
World, now spread
throughout the globe.*

cigarette-making machine in the 1880s made increased production possible. This happened to coincide with the beginning of most of the aggressive selling techniques we know today.

It was not only the convenience of the cigarette that made its advent so important a landmark. A new type of tobacco had become available in the United States in the mid-19th century— a mild variety that was flue-cured (i.e., dried quickly in warmed barns rather than slowly in the sun). Most historians have overlooked the fact that, with the type of tobaccos used in pipes and cigars, the nicotine was largely absorbed through contact with the tissues in the mouth and throat. The smoke was too acrid to inhale. The nicotine in the new, milder, more acidic tobaccos was poorly absorbed from the mouth, but the smoke was mild enough to inhale. Thus, despite the lower nicotine content of cigarette tobacco, a cigarette actually delivered more nicotine to the brain of the smoker—and did so with quite amazing rapidity.

In a few decades, the sales of cigarettes in the United States soared from millions to billions to hundreds of billions. Even more startling is that this increase took place despite an active anti-tobacco movement that succeeded in pushing cigarette prohibition laws through the legislatures of more than 14 states.

It is apparent that neither extremely high costs, nor moral pronouncements (whether by princes or popes), nor draconian penalties (up to and including death), nor fears of adverse medical effects have been able to snuff out man's desire for tobacco. Some of these measures and conditions certainly retarded the rate at which the use of tobacco spread, but it seems that no society which has begun to use tobacco has ever completely given it up.[1]

Why do people smoke?

In response to this question, most smokers give many reasons for their behaviour. Researchers tend to break the question down into four separate parts:

What causes people to try smoking in the first place?
What makes them become confirmed smokers?
Why do they have such great difficulty giving up the practice, even when convinced that it is injuring their health?
What causes so many former smokers to relapse after a successful effort to stop?

'I need something to do with my hands...'

82

There is general agreement that people begin to smoke for one or more of the following reasons: curiosity; to conform to the norms of a group to which they want to belong; to express rebellion; and to imitate the behaviour of people who appear to have greater status, as in the case of young people wishing to appear more 'grown-up'.

There is less agreement on exactly what determines which experimenters with tobacco will become regular or confirmed smokers, why people do not stop smoking when they say they want to, and why people relapse after a period of abstinence.

Why smokers continue to smoke

According to one well known study, six major factors appear to influence smokers to continue to smoke:[1] stimulation—getting a sense of increased energy; sensorimotor manipulation—getting satisfaction from handling and lighting the cigarettes; pleasurable relaxation—rewarding oneself with a cigarette after the need to

A love-hate relationship.

stay alert and tense has passed, or to enhance social interaction; habit—the smoker doesn't miss cigarettes if they are not available, but smokes automatically if they are, and does not think that they make him feel any different; reduction of negative affect—smoking in order to cope with feelings of tension, anxiety, or anger in difficult situations; and addiction—smoking to prevent the unpleasant sense of craving that being without cigarettes produces.

'Tension reduction' and 'addiction' seem to be the two most important of these according to smokers themselves.[2]

Who becomes a smoker?

The most important factors determining who becomes a smoker are the availability of tobacco and the social context in which smoking begins. Smokers tend to have other smokers as friends, and a person is far more likely to smoke if there is a parent or sibling in the family who also smokes. Smokers appear to put a higher value on the meaning placed on the act of smoking in their own families, social class, and circle of friends than on potential long-term effects. Higher educational attainment generally means less propensity to smoke. Rich women are more likely to smoke than poor ones, but rich men are less likely to do so than poor ones.

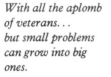

With all the aplomb of veterans. . . but small problems can grow into big ones.

Smokers, even as teenagers, tend to be more impulsive, more adventurous, more social, more rebellious, and less tolerant of restrictions and authority. They drink more coffee, tea, and alcohol than non-smokers, are found to use more marijuana,

amphetamines, barbiturates, and other illicit drugs (a non-smoker who is a heavy user of illicit drugs is a relative rarity).

Smokers start to drink alcohol and to engage in sexual activity at an earlier age. They may weigh a few pounds less than non-smokers, even though they consume more calories per day; and they are also rather more anxious and angrier. There is great overlap between smokers and non-smokers, however. Differences between them emerge only when hundreds of cases are studied.[2]

Personality differences between smokers and non-smokers are probably due to a combination of environment and heredity. Environmental factors are self-evident. An hereditary factor is

Smoking is sophisticated... that's the message.

suggested by the finding that when identical twins (who have exactly the same genetic endowment) are raised apart, they tend to have similar smoking habits more often than non-identical twins raised apart. It seems the way we meet stress and react to the world is (at least in part) determined genetically. Those who become regular smokers obviously find the effects of tobacco more beneficial or more pleasurable than others.

The attractions of nicotine

Is it primarily the effect of the drug, nicotine, that gives tobacco its great appeal? If so, just what is it about nicotine that makes it so precious to its users?

In 1942, a British researcher, Dr Lennox Johnston, used injections of nicotine as a substitute for smoking in 35 volunteer subjects. Non-smokers found injected nicotine unpleasant, but, if the doses were adequate, smokers did not feel the need to smoke for some time afterwards. In a similar experiment in 1978 conducted by Reese Jones and his co-workers, smokers again found nicotine injections pleasant; non-smokers experienced nausea.

In another early experiment, a group of smokers were given alternately low-nicotine and normal-nicotine cigarettes without knowing which were which. Half of them did not notice any change in their sense of wellbeing or experienced only a vague lack of their normal satisfaction while on low nicotine. A few definitely missed the nicotine but adapted after a week or two, and about a third missed the nicotine throughout the period of several weeks, with 'varying degrees of heightened irritableness, decreased ability to concentrate on mental tasks, a feeling of inner hunger or emptiness . . . .'

The conclusion—that nicotine is what smokers smoke for—is supported by a 1967 trial in which subjects received an intravenous injection of either nicotine or saline solution. With nicotine, their smoking rate dropped over a quarter; but it was not affected by the saline. Since then, many experiments have shown that when the nicotine level in a smoker's cigarette is reduced the pattern of smoking is altered to compensate. This finding has important implications for those who switch to low nicotine cigarettes. In all likelihood, these compensatory mechanisms result in their taking far more tar, nicotine and carbon monoxide than the labels on the cigarettes would imply.[3]

Nicotine is a relatively short-acting drug, and its levels in the bloodstream decline quickly (to about half within 30 minutes of finishing a cigarette and to only a quarter within another half hour). It is no coincidence that most smokers use about 20 cigarettes over the 16 waking hours of the day.

Yet smoking obviously involves more than just maintaining the body's nicotine level. In terms of its effects on mood and

Keeping on your toes?

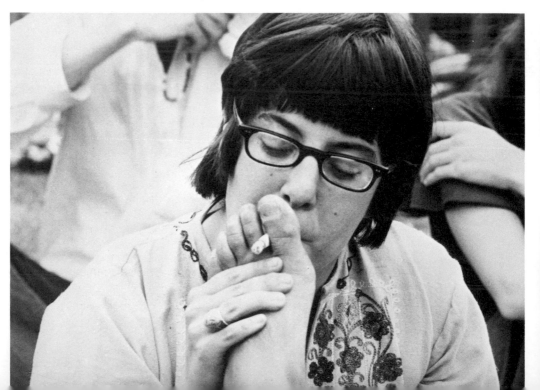

behaviour, nicotine given by mouth as capsules or in the form of chewing gum or even by injection cannot reliably substitute for nicotine obtained by inhaling tobacco smoke into the lungs.[3]

What nicotine does

Nicotine produces changes in the nervous system, the endocrine system, the blood vessels and the gastrointestinal system. Multiple changes are produced within the nervous system.

Nicotine makes the heart beat faster and elevates blood pressure. This is thought to be partly due to the release of adrenaline from the adrenal glands. Nicotine is known to affect the brain in a similar way to a substance called acetylcholine, which transmits nerve inpulses from one neuron to another, and some researchers believe that nicotine releases the neurotransmitter substance noradrenaline from nerve cells in the brain. It also seems to release noradrenaline from the nerve cells supplying the heart. It is known to produce a release of several hormones from the pituitary gland.[2,3,4]

In tiny doses, nicotine increases the activity of inhibitory (Renshaw) cells in the spinal cord, which causes a decrease in muscle tone. The kind of muscle relaxation produced differs from that produced by other drugs such as barbiturates or minor tranquillisers. Brain wave patterns show an increase in alertness similar to that produced by amphetamine. Smokers often report that an increased sense of energy and ability to concentrate accompanies their feeling of relaxation.[2,4] However, we cannot be sure that such nicotine effects are necessarily relevant to *smoking behaviour*.

The effects of tobacco may depend to some extent on the person who uses it. Some smokers feel that it is a stimulant and helps them cope with boredom. Others feel that tobacco helps them blot out distracting environmental stimuli and reduce inner feelings of anxiety, tension and irritability.

Smoking and anger

One of the more intriguing areas of current research examines the effects of nicotine on irritability, anger and aggression.

In one set of experiments, monkeys were put in a situation where they were unable to escape an electric shock to their tails. As the time for the shock approached, the animals tended to increase their manipulation of levers in the cage. Immediately after the shock they bit on a rubber tube.

The experimenters recorded the intensity, duration and frequency of the biting, as well as the frequency of pre-shock lever responses. Doses of nicotine tended to increase the response before the shock and to decrease the biting after it. In studies of the effects of repeated, long-term nicotine administration, it was found that when the drug was abruptly withdrawn there was a sharp increase in the post-shock biting attacks. This lasted for about two days, after which the biting behaviour fell back to pre-drug levels.

Similar experiments were also conducted on human volunteers, using loud sounds rather than shocks, and recording electrical activity in the jaw muscles rather than biting. Nicotine reduced jaw muscle tension even in non-smokers, and smokers showed a temporary increase in jaw tension for a week or two after giving up smoking.[5]

'Ah, but I don't inhale!'

Rapid action of nicotine

A drug that increases the likelihood of its own self-administration is described by behavioural psychologists as a 'reinforcer' of drug-taking behaviour. Nicotine appears to be a relatively weak reinforcer of drug-taking behaviour in man and animals. But it may compensate for this weakness in other ways.

Each puff of smoke drawn into contact with the vast capillary bed of the lungs delivers a small dose of nicotine to the brain more rapidly than the dose of heroin that an addict shoots into an arm vein. The more rapidly a behaviour is followed by a positive effect, the more effectively it is reinforced. Each inhaled puff can thus be regarded as a potential reinforcer of puffing behaviour. There are about 10 puffs in each cigarette and a heavy smoker consumes more than 20 cigarettes a day. Even after only a year or two, the act of inhalation has been reinforced more than 100,000 times.

If physical dependence on nicotine develops, it is likely that each small dose of nicotine produces its own relatively mild reinforcement by relieving the nicotine withdrawal syndrome. This relief may be even more reinforcing than the original effect of nicotine itself.[3,4]

Is smoking an addiction?

If 'addiction' means an overwhelming compulsion or need to continue to use a pharmacological substance, then some smokers are clearly addicted to tobacco. If addiction means a change in the body produced by giving a drug over and over again, so that when it is stopped there is a definable withdrawal syndrome, then again some smokers are addicted. However, if by addiction we mean a drug-induced change in the body so severe that some users die or become extremely ill when the drug is stopped, then tobacco is not an addicting substance. There has never been a recorded death from abrupt cessation of tobacco.

Many scholars maintain that the true measure of drug addiction as a behaviour is the extent a user will go to get the drug, how much its use takes precedence over other values in life, and to what extent the user can control the use. They also maintain that a withdrawal syndrome can, without threatening life itself, profoundly affect behaviour.[2,3]

A cigarette can be a temporary comfort in acute situations...

Withdrawal of opioid drugs is rarely life-threatening, but many opioid users make considerable sacrifices—sometimes risking life and freedom—to see that they have adequate supplies.

And can relax the camera-shy!

Risking all for tobacco

Many smokers also make great sacrifices and take great risks to maintain a supply of tobacco. When the occupation of Holland during World War II led to widespread starvation in some of the cities, many preferred to grow tobacco rather than vegetables in their garden allotments. Even meagre concentration camp food was exchanged for cigarettes.

Most doctors have come across patients whose limbs had been amputated because of tobacco-induced peripheral vascular disease, yet who continued to chain-smoke. Other patients adamantly refuse to give up cigarettes even after surgery for cancer requiring the creation of a tracheostomy (an opening through the neck in to the windpipe). They draw the smoke directly into the lungs through the tracheostomy.

Some of the controversy surrounding tobacco (or nicotine) as an addicting substance is possibly due to the fact that as many as half of all smokers are able to give up smoking with only mild and transient discomfort or even no discomfort at all. Such reasoning, however, could be falsely applied to alcohol, since many who use it regularly can stop using it with only mild discomfort. If similar logic is extended, one could say that opioids do not cause dependence (in anyone) because so many opioid users can stop on their own.

The issue is not whether every smoker is addicted, any more than it is whether every regular drinker is an alcoholic. There are many who, given what they feel are adequate reasons, can give up either drug. But is it clear that the claim of many smokers that 'I can stop any time I want to' is no more valid than that of the alcoholic who makes the identical statement.

Many experts now feel that we should substitute the word 'dependence' for the term 'addiction'. Tobacco produces a dependence. About that there can be no dispute.[2, 3, 4]

The earlier you start,
the harder it is to stop.

Giving it up: what happens?

There is surprisingly strong resistance to the idea of a nicotine withdrawal syndrome, despite ample documentation of a fairly consistent pattern of symptoms which emerge when heavy smokers are deprived of tobacco. While they may vary from smoker to smoker, the most widely reported are irritability, bad temper, restlessness, nervousness, drowsiness, lightheadedness, energy loss, fatigue, insomnia, inability to concentrate, tremor, palpitations and headache.

Physiological changes occur with greater consistency. They include a lowering of pulse rate and diastolic blood pressure. The intensity of the withdrawal syndrome seems to reach its peak within the first day or two, and then declines sharply over a few days. Some former smokers claim that the craving and some of the other withdrawal symptoms, such as irritability and inability to concentrate, may persist for weeks or months.[2]

The finding that excessive irritability is commonly reported as a tobacco withdrawal syndrome is particularly fascinating since nicotine has been found in some laboratory studies to be effective in reducing feelings of anger and frustration. Furthermore, those who become heavy smokers tended to be angrier and less tolerant of frustration, rules and authority than light smokers and non-smokers in the first place. The heavy smoker possibly finds it hard to tolerate the sharp increase in angry feelings during withdrawal. It could be that those who experience more than the average amount of anger or frustration have found in tobacco a useful non-sedating tranquilliser. Obviously, it comes with too many side effects.

91

Stopping and starting again

Whether we call it a habit, an addiction, or dependence, it is clear that many smokers simply refuse to give up smoking. Others say they want to stop, but make no effort to do so. Still others have tried and failed—others have tried, were successful for a time, and then relapsed.

Gambling with tension—and smoking to relax. The paradox of human behaviour.

In the United States there are more than 30 million former smokers. A little more than a decade ago, about 60 per cent of United States physicians were smokers; the proportion is now about 21 per cent. Yet these statistics of success cannot mask the sad fact that a heavy smoker who feels the need for some formal help to give up smoking has only a modest prospect of long-term success.

The average results of a large number of smoking cessation programmes show that more than half of those who were initially successful in stopping begin smoking again within six months. By the twelfth month, only 25–35 per cent of those who stopped are still non-smokers.

Those who seek help to give up cigarettes may not be representative of all smokers. Some experts believe that these are the heaviest smokers; others feel they represent the best motivated heavy smokers. Nevertheless, for such a smoker, there is less than one chance in five that one effort at treatment using current approaches will be enough.

'This time I'm really stopping. Really!'

Helping smokers give up

The treatments that have been offered to help smokers kick the habit range from hypnosis to aversive conditioning, in which electric shocks or hot smoky air blown in the smoker's face are linked with the act of smoking. They also include acupuncture and the use of other drugs to substitute for the effects of nicotine or to relieve the effects of tobacco withdrawal. These are discussed in Chapter 10.

It is interesting that, despite the role that nicotine plays in perpetuating the smoking habit, it is difficult to prove that pharmacological substitutes, including nicotine chewing gums or aerosols, are any better than non-pharmacological methods in helping smokers to stop.

The high relapse rate is probably a result of a combination of factors, including the easy availability of cigarettes, and continued smoking by friends and relatives. Many smokers undoubtedly miss smoking for the very reasons that they became smokers in the first place. The drug effect produced a pleasurable state of stimulation or relaxation that helped them adjust to the demands and stresses of life.

So a former smoker not only has to deal with his or her original 'inner need' for the effects of tobacco, but also with some of the results of tobacco smoking. It is quite likely that, in the course of years of smoking, many aspects of the behaviour and of the nicotine withdrawal syndrome have become conditioned or linked to elements of the smoker's environment. As a result, the environment can provoke conditioned withdrawal symptoms which the smoker experiences as an intense sense of craving for a cigarette. It can take months or years before these conditioned responses are extinguished or die out.[2]

The killer

Concern about the effects of smoking began when scientists became alarmed at the remarkable increase in the death rate due to lung cancer. Even the earliest studies indicated a clear association between cigarette smoking and lung cancer. More detailed studies not only confirmed a higher death rate among smokers, but revealed that only one-eighth of the extra deaths were due to lung cancer.

The remainder were due to coronary heart disease (CHD), chronic (non-cancerous) diseases of the lung, and other forms of cancer. The excess deaths occurred mainly among cigarette smokers, and the death rate among those who used cigars or pipes was only slightly greater than that of non-smokers.[2]

Those early suspicions of clinicians and pathologists has now been clearly established. Early development of coronary heart disease is the major consequence of heavy cigarette smoking. Smokers have a greater chance of having a heart attack and less chance of surviving one than non-smokers. Long-term cigarette smokers are twice as likely to die of coronary heart diseases as non-smokers.

In the United States, more than 600,000 deaths each year are due to coronary heart disease. It is the leading cause of death. At least a third of these deaths are attributable to cigarette smoking. Many countries have a lower rate of CHD than the United States, but smoking still sharply increases the risk. And that increase is greater in proportion to the amount smoked.

A lesser known but hardly less dramatic and painful disease of the cardiovascular system is *arteriosclerosis obliterans*. This causes obstruction of the arteries carrying blood to the limbs, leading to the development of gangrene and possible amputation rather than sudden death. Men who smoke more than 20 cigarettes a day are nine times more likely to develop the disease than are non-smokers. Women on more than 20 a day are 15 times more likely to develop it.

The link with cancer

Lung cancer is the second most important health risk associated with cigarette smoking and most people are now fully aware of the link. In the United States, where 84,000 people die of lung cancer each year, the risk of lung cancer for 20-a-day smokers is ten times as great as it is for non-smokers. Among Japanese men who smoke, the risk is nine times as great; but, if they smoke more than 50 cigarettes a day, it is 25 times as high.

The risk of cancer of the throat, mouth and vocal chords is also substantially elevated for smokers, and increases with the number of cigarettes smoked daily and the number of years of smoking. It is less well known, but nevertheless indisputable, that smokers also have increased chance of developing cancer of the pancreas and bladder.

Cigarettes have been blamed for most of the major medical problems, especially those that lead to death. However, those who smoke pipes and cigars do run a substantially higher risk of developing cancers of the lip, tongue, jaw, throat, and oesophagus than do non-smokers.[2]

Other risks
As well as the diseases of the heart and blood vessels, and malignant (cancerous) disease of the lung and other organs, smoking also causes a number of serious non-malignant disorders of the respiratory system. Cigarette smoking is believed to be the most important cause of emphysema, in which the air sacs of the lungs become distended because of chronic obstruction of the bronchial passages. In the United States, emphysema kills more than 20,000 people each year. Smoking is also a major cause of chronic bronchitis.

The smoker is not only personally affected by the habit.

Cigarette smoking during the last six months of pregnancy creates a higher risk of miscarriage, stillbirth, and of new-born death. Otherwise healthy babies of mothers who smoke during pregnancy tend to have lower average birth weights than babies of non-smokers, and, during the first year of life, children of parents who smoke have a much higher rate of respiratory infections.

Knowledge is not enough

Educational campaigns have made the adverse medical effects of smoking common knowledge. Most people agree that smoking is harmful and frequently causes disease and death. Yet the number of smokers continues to rise. Between 1968 and 1974, the proportion of regular smokers among men in their late teens remained steady at about 28 per cent, but the rate of cigarette smoking among young women actually rose from 18 per cent to 25 per cent. Lung cancer and heart disease in women is now rising rapidly, reflecting this increase in smokers.[2]

The number of cigarettes produced annually has continued to grow in the United States, and by 1973 the figures exceeded 600 billion cigarettes. This is slightly more than 4,000 cigarettes a year for every person over the age of 18. If there is any glimmer of hope in these gloomy statistics, it is that *per capita* consumption in the United States has been relatively flat since the Surgeon General's report of 1964 linking cigarettes with lung cancer. The growth in total consumption is due primarily to the population growth, and during the past four years there has been a decline in the proportion of adult males who smoke—to about 39 per cent from an all-time high of almost 60 per cent.[2]

What can be done?

There are now some signs that governmental inertia is giving way to action on the effects on health of tobacco. In some countries, taxes have been raised and advertising has been banned. But the real solutions are still far from clear. The use of tobacco spread long before advertising and at a time when it cost relatively far more than it does today, even under proposed new tax schedules. Simple attempts to ban tobacco without knowing why it is so enjoyed by so many seem to be doomed. If we can find out exactly why it gives some of us 'a certain secret pleasure', perhaps we can find a less destructive way to get the effects we now get from tobacco.

*"But can I last till
Friday?"*

9 Alcohol and alcoholism

'I couldn't see no snakes, but he said they was crawling up his legs; and then he would give a jump and scream and say one had bit him on the cheek. I never see a man look so wild. Pretty soon he was all fagged out, and fell down panting; then he rolled over and over, screaming and saying there was devils a-hold of him. . . . By and by he raised up part way and listened with his head to one side. He wails, very low:

'Tramp—tramp—tramp; that's the dead; tramp—tramp—tramp; they're coming after me; but I won't go. Oh, they're here! Don't touch me—don't. Hands off—they're cold; let go. Oh, let a poor devil alone!"

He rolled himself up in his blanket and went on crying.'

Huckleberry Finn describing his father.

Although the kind of delirious state experienced by Huck's drunkard father can sometimes occur during withdrawal from alcohol, it is quite rare. But it is at the heart of the layman's conception of problem drinking or alcoholism. Yet a far more common face of problem drinking is a less dramatic kind affecting millions throughout the world.

Many people who vigorously resist the label 'alcoholic' have lost some degree of control over alcohol in one way or another, and many of them would like to give it up entirely, or at least regain control. This applies as much to the family man whose wife and children are turning against him because he drinks too much as to the lonely widow who has lost friends because of her excessive drinking and its distressing consequences.

These people have 'a drink problem'—they would like to drink less but cannot. To a greater or lesser extent they have lost their freedom of choice and are, whatever euphemisms we may use, 'alcohol dependent'. Not everyone whose drinking causes problems is an alcoholic. Some people drink and get into trouble while driving and although this is a problem that merits attention, it is not necessarily related to alcoholism.

Origins and effects

Since at least 6,000 BC beers and wines have been produced through the fermenting action of yeast fungi on certain sugars. It was not until 800 AD that ethyl alcohol, the effective ingredient of alcoholic drinks, was produced in a more concentrated form. It is thought that an Arab known as Jahir ibn Hayyan invented the process of distillation and was the first to make a more potent drink similar in its effects to brandy or vodka.

Most bars throughout the world now stock a large variety of alcoholic beverages with different concentrations of ethyl alcohol (C_2H_5OH). The main types, their alcohol content and method of production are displayed in the table below.

Production and content of alcoholic beverages

Group	Example of specific beverages	Alcohol content % v/v	Production
Beers	Lager Ales Stout	3–6 3–6 4–8	Brewer's wort fermented by yeast with hops as flavouring
Table wines	Still: red, white, and rosé	8–14	Fermentation of crushed grapes or grape juice
	Sparkling: champagne	12	Second fermentation with retention of carbon dioxide
Dessert and cocktail wines	Sherry, port, madeira, vermouth	15–20	Ordinary wines plus added brandy or high proof spirit and plant extracts as flavouring
Distilled spirits	Brandy	40	Direct distillation of fermented grape mash
	Whisky	37–40	Double distillation of fermented barley or corn mash
	Rum	40	Distillation of fermented molasses
	Gin	37–40	Tasteless distillate flavoured by second distillation with berries, etc.
	Vodka	37·5	Distillation of grain
Liqueurs	Benedictine, chartreuse, kirsch	20–55	Neutral spirits plus flavouring

A moderate dose of alcohol stimulates circulation and can give us a warm feeling on a cold winter's day. However, a larger dose tends to reduce body temperature because of its action on the temperature-regulating mechanism in the brain. The sight of a St Bernard with a keg of brandy hanging from its collar may be a comfort to the shivering climber, but in fact a dose of brandy only has a transient warming effect and may actually reduce body temperature.

Of course, one of the main reasons for the popularity of alcohol is its effect on the central nervous system. A small or moderate dose appears to stimulate. Social gatherings tend to come alive, the introvert become more extroverted, and people tend to be rather more assertive and even aggressive.

The stimulating effect of alcohol is the result of disinhibition. Anxieties and fears which sometimes suppress behaviour tend to be reduced, so that the intoxicated person is less likely to be influenced by possible unpleasant consequences.

How drunk is drunk?

From a number of experiments on human subjects, we can delineate a very rough relationship between blood alcohol levels and the various effects of alcohol. At blood levels of about 50mg, many people tend to be a little more relaxed and carefree. Even at such a low level there is an effect on psychomotor tasks; reaction times are increased and driving skills affected.

'Give us another, Jerry, I'm just getting relaxed!'

At 80mg, driving tends to be seriously impaired. Most people become very clumsy and emotionally labile at levels of 100mg and movements are severely affected at 200mg. Ninety per cent

of people are very intoxicated at 300mg and dead at levels above 500mg.

The experimental work also indicates, however, that there are large variations in people's responses to alcohol, depending upon mood, personality, beliefs about alcohol, as well as past drinking habits, and the situation or setting in which drink is consumed. It is also clear that although alcohol is often consumed in order to obtain its disinhibitory effects, there are many other factors which strongly influence drinking, including social imitation, social approval, price and availability.

Interactions with other drugs

Most people consider a drug to be either a substance prescribed by doctors or a narcotic sought after by drug addicts. Alcohol is not usually considered to be a medicine, but it is also a drug. It has dose-related effects on the central nervous system and causes physiological changes in the brain which lead to physiological dependence.

Care must be taken when using alcohol along with other drugs. It is usually called a central nervous system depressant and its effects will be enhanced by other drugs having a similar sedative action, such as barbiturates and minor tranquillisers, like Librium and Valium. An overdose of barbiturates is particularly dangerous when taken with alcohol.

Psychology of a drinker

'*Think what you like*': *disapproval can have the opposite effect to the one desired.*

Whether a social drinker or an alcoholic will drink on a particular occasion, and how much, depends on a number of factors. Among them are the level of stress or threat to the drinker, the expected consequences of drinking, the social context and his or her commitment to a particular intake of alcohol. There are now numerous experimental studies which demonstrate that heavy drinkers will increase their consumption if exposed to criticism or the threat of critical appraisal.[1]

Drinking, like much other behaviour, is powerfully influenced by modelling—that is, by the behaviour of other people. An alcoholic on a prolonged drinking bout has been known to put a stop to his drinking, after 16 days, simply because his companion had stopped. It has been shown experimentally that heavy social drinkers who observed a 'model' drinking very heavily consumed more wine than subjects who had either seen a 'model' just sipping lightly or had been given no modelling at all.

During treatment, those social pressures which tempt an alcoholic to break his abstinence are particularly important. Relapse has been closely related to this kind of pressure, and some therapists include a special 'Say No' course in their treatment.

The layman often believes that there is an 'alcoholic personality' which is clearly identifiable and particularly vulnerable. In fact, such a personality has never been identified. Since the development of a drinking problem is a very complex function of personality and environmental factors, it is unlikely that an alcoholic personality trait will ever be identified.

Some people drink for excitement, others to reduce anxiety. Some drink in order to be one of the boys and others to punish their wives. To search for *the* alcoholic personality is like looking for *the* cause of heart disease or *the* cause of automobile breakdowns. Nevertheless, there is evidence that many people with drinking problems use drink in order to reduce anxiety.

The relaxing effect of alcohol was the downfall of this alcoholic musician:

> I was desperate for something to calm the now shattered nervous system and I accepted his proffered glass of scotch. The effect was instantaneous ... and it worked. From that moment on, I was never to be without a bottle on any engagement I undertook, and this state lasted for the next 20 years. ... I made a pact with the stuff: 'I'll drink you and you take my nerves away'.

Even rats get Dutch courage from a dose of alcohol. If a rat is given an electric shock as it walks along a corridor towards a food box, it experiences an approach-avoidance conflict. It has been shown that the avoidance and fear can be reduced by a moderate dose of alcohol.

Social setting for a drink

The decision to drink is the result of a complex interaction between the drinker and his social environment. Many investigations have clearly demonstrated that heavy drinking is strongly influenced by one's sex, ethnic group, occupation and country, as well as price and availability. One survey confirmed that drinking problems differ with ethno-religious groupings: most Jewish men drink, but few of them drink heavily or get into trouble because of their drinking; most Catholics and liberal Protestants drink, and an above average proportion have drinking problems—whereas conservative, or 'puritan', Protestants (from denominations favouring total abstinence) show a high proportion of abstainers, although the heavy drinkers among them frequently have problems.[2]

A disproportionate number of heavy drinkers live in the wine-producing countries, probably because drink is freely available and drinking an incidental part of everyday living. The generally permissive attitude towards drinking influences the drinking habits of individuals and the social policies of governments.

Occupations, too, play a part in the tendency to drink heavily; company directors, publicans and inn-keepers, stage managers, actors, entertainers, musicians, cooks and seamen have a high death rate from alcohol, including cirrhosis of the liver. We do

What's a wedding without a drink or two? Tradition reinforces drinking patterns.

not fully understand why these groups tend to drink heavily, but it has been suggested that relevant factors include the availability of drink, social pressure to drink—or, looking at it from the other side, the selection of drink-related occupations by people who are already heavy drinkers.

Price and availability

A number of behavioural scientists believe increased taxation would, at a stroke, reduce the prevalence of alcoholism, drinking problems and liver cirrhosis. The availability of alcohol, certainly influences the number of heavy drinkers in a population.

Hard as it is to believe from the movies and novels of the time, deaths from liver cirrhosis dropped significantly during the prohibition era in the United States and there was a similar change in France during the Second World War when the supply of wine was drastically reduced. People simply drank less. By contrast, when the Finnish government relaxed restrictions on the sale of beer in stores and eating places recently, alcohol consumption increased by about half within a year.

Alcohol dependence

The case against heavy drinking is not, of course, just the damage it does to the body. There are stronger poisons by far. It is the fact that it can create a dependence in those who use it, allied with its injuriousness, that makes it so dangerous.

Central to the theory of addiction are the concepts of tolerance and physical dependence. Tolerance refers to the tendency of the central nervous system to adapt to the intoxicating effects of a drug so that a larger dose is needed to produce the same effect. Tolerance of alcohol is displayed not only by the heavy social drinker who boasts that he can drink his friends under the table, or by the severely dependent alcoholic who can consume half a bottle of whisky without appearing to be intoxicated, but also by rats given daily doses of 6gm per kg of body weight over a two week period.

Physical dependence has been defined by the World Health Organisation as 'an adaptive state that manifests itself by intense physical disturbance when the administration of the drug is suspended'. The parallel development of tolerance and physical dependence lead to an increased level of consumption, since a large dose of alcohol is needed to produce the same effect and also drinking is likely to be continued in order to avoid actual or expected withdrawal symptoms. So the person who is severely dependent on alcohol is both psychologically and physiologically dependent, and is suffering from the alcohol dependence syndrome. This syndrome has been described in the following way:[3]

First, there is a subjective awareness of a compulsion to drink so that drinking takes priority over other activities. Drink becomes more important than one's family, job, friends and health. There is a narrowing of the drinking repertoire so that the more dependent a person becomes, the more stereotyped his drinking behaviour.

Tolerance to alcohol increases and withdrawal symptoms such as shakiness, sweats and depression tend to occur, especially on the morning after the night before when blood alcohol levels are drastically reduced. Frequently drink is consumed in order to escape and avoid withdrawal symptoms, these symptoms typically disappearing very rapidly after a few drinks. Bottles are hidden away at home or at work so that the alcoholic is always prepared for the sudden onset of withdrawal symptoms. Finally, if the severely dependent alcoholic is able to remain abstinent, he is still at risk. There is a strong possibility that if he starts drinking again, he will lapse into his old habits within a few days.

A vicious circle

The emergence of physical dependence is important in the development of alcoholism, but does not fully explain it. The severly dependent alcoholic is at the mercy of both physical and psychological processes. Typically, somebody who already drinks heavily and finds that drink reduces social tensions will, in any socially tense situation, come to experience a compulsion to drink. This amounts to psychological dependence. Continued heavy drinking will also bring about physical dependence, which carries with it its own reinforcement in the shape of upsetting and even horrific withdrawal symptoms if drinking is stopped. Thus a cycle is built up—social tensions provide a cue for

*A few drinks can
make for a good time—*

drinking, reluctance to face withdrawal provides a cue for
continuing to drink.

Defining alcoholism

Although hundreds of books have been written on the subject
and millions of people have asked, 'Is my husband (or wife) an
alcoholic?', the exact definition of alcoholism is still debated.
There is usually agreement when the dependence is severe and
most of the components of the alcohol dependence syndrome are
clearly present. But there is no sharp point at which a heavy
drinker suddenly becomes an alcoholic.

Alcohol dependence is not an all or none phenomenon but, like
deafness or fatness, it is present in degrees. When do we say that
a person is deaf rather than hard of hearing? At what point do we
say that a person is obese rather than plump? Because alcohol
dependence is a continuum ranging from slight to severe, there
is nothing to be gained from agreeing on a cut-off point above
which the heavy drinker is alcoholic and below which he is just
a problem drinker.

If you are wondering whether a member of your family, or a
close relative, is an alcoholic, then ask yourself instead: Is his
drinking gradually increasing from year to year? Does his
frequent heavy drinking lead on to unpleasant psychological,
social and physical consequences such as family arguments,
accidents or problems at work? Do the various components of

the alcohol dependence syndrome apply to him? Does he frequently drink to relax and forget his worries?

If the answer is 'yes' to most of these questions then your friend or relative is more or less dependent on alcohol and should think seriously about his drinking habits and his future. If he cannot return to moderate drinking or abstinence as a result of his own efforts, then perhaps he should contact his doctor or Alcoholics Anonymous and explore the possibility that he can get some help from others. If drinking problems are viewed in this way, then it doesn't matter whether we use the label 'alcoholic'.

Alcohol and mental state

Although alcohol can enhance pleasant feelings for a few hours, prolonged ingestion nearly always leads to a gradual deterioration in mood. After a few days, the heavy drinker will begin to feel more depressed and irritable. He may have difficulty facing other people, and becomes prey to gloomy and suspicious thoughts.

Many drinkers do not attribute these feelings to alcohol and if their drinking history is not disclosed, a medical practitioner could well compound the problem by prescribing tranquillisers which simply add to the effects of alcohol and exacerbate any depression.

Sometimes the heavy drinker does not realise, but more often he knows full well, that his personality is not attractive to others when he is intoxicated. Many social, vocational and marital problems are caused by the disinhibitory effects of drink. The alcoholic often gets a reputation for silly, inappropriate talk and for an aggressive manner which can soon ruin a previously happy relationship.

It is commonly believed that alcohol is an aphrodisiac, but in fact many alcoholics suffer from impotence. Alcohol 'provokes the desire, but it takes away the performance'—according to the porter in Macbeth. There is some evidence that this temporary impotence in men may cause enough worry to promote the condition even when they are not drunk.

But alcohol can also bring out hidden personality problems.

Memory blackouts, alcoholic hallucinosis, delirium tremens and withdrawal fits are all very unpleasant consequences of heavy drinking. The alcoholic may find it impossible to recall exactly what he was doing the night before, even though he was conscious or even animated for most of the time. Such blackouts were once thought to be a certain sign of alcoholism, but we now know that although it is a very serious sign, it is quite a common experience for the heavy drinker.

Delirium tremens or DTs of the type experienced by Huckleberry Finn's father is an extreme manifestation of the alcohol abstinence syndrome, developing within a few days of withdrawal. Withdrawal fits are also extreme forms of the abstinence syndrome and may occur after about 24 hours without drink. The heavy drinker who starts to hear voices is probably not suffering from schizophrenia but from alcoholic hallucinosis.

Depression and suicide are almost as common among alcoholics as among people with pure depressive disorder. In some cases the depression may be part of the reason for drinking, but in others it may actually be a result of heavy alcohol use and may be alleviated by abstinence.

Alcohol and the body

Liver cirrhosis is such a common consequence of prolonged heavy drinking that cirrhosis rates are often used as an index of a country's drinking problem. There is now enough evidence to suggest that drinking between five and ten pints of beer or more each day, or an equivalent amount of wine and spirits, increases the risk of cirrhosis. Some research reports have suggested that more than 80 per cent of people who drink ten pints or more are likely to suffer from liver damage.

Stomach and duodenal ulcers are also linked to alcohol consumption, and more than 20 per cent with alcoholism have some kind of ulceration.

The severely dependent alcoholic risks brain damage and intellectual impairment, chiefly of learning ability and memory. This befuddlement, called Korsakoff's syndrome, is usually the result of years of excessive drinking.

The fetal alcohol syndrome is now being intensively studied in the United States. There is evidence to suggest that a pregnant woman who drinks heavily is probably causing physical harm to her unborn child. Such a baby might suffer from mild or moderate mental retardation, with an abnormally small head, congenital heart disease and other congenital deformities.

So alcohol, like any other drug, can cause enormous mental and physical damage if taken in excess.[4] Add together the increased risks of developing liver cirrhosis, ulcers, cancer and brain damage, as well as the increased risk of accidents, self-poisoning and violence, and it would appear that the life expectancy of a heavy drinker is likely to be drastically reduced. In one British study, a group of 935 patients were followed up ten to 15 years after admission to a hospital with the diagnosis of alcoholism. It was found that a mortality rate for this group was about 300 per cent above that expected for the general population.

Social problems

Public drunkenness is a punishable offence mainly because the disinhibited drunk is frequently a public nuisance and is likely to be overtly aggressive. There are now over 100,000 convictions for drunkenness in England and Wales every year—resulting in about 3,000 prison sentences. Many of these are petty offences, but alcohol has also been implicated in a high proportion of more

The habitual drunkard is a common sight, but not a pretty one.

distressing crimes of violence, from murder to football hooliganism. The notion that alcohol releases inhibitions has been applied equally to aggressive sexual behaviour. About half of committed rapists and paedophiles had been drinking when they committed their offences.

It has been claimed that alcoholism in industry in the United States costs $10 billion a year although, because of difficulties in measuring the prevalence of drinking problems, this can only be considered to be a rough guide. For the United Kingdom, £40 million a year has been quoted, with £20 million paid out in sickness benefit. Apart from the excessive cost to society and the health cost to the drinker himself, people in the alcoholic's immediate environment sometimes have to put up with almost intolerable experiences.

A family problem

Most families with an alcoholic member are going to suffer in the short term and probably for years after the drinking problem subsides. But not enough research has been done to offer more than a few generalisations based on empirical observations. Most of this research has been on the families of male alcoholics: very little is known about the impact of an alcoholic wife on family dynamics. Similarly, there has been a lot of speculation about the children of alcoholic parents but relatively little good research.

It has been found that the wives of alcoholics are in general more disturbed than the rest of the population: but whether this means that the alcoholic husband has caused the disturbance, or that disturbed women tend to marry alcoholics, is not clear. The former is, on present evidence, the more likely.

It is widely believed that the children of alcoholics face a high risk of developing alcoholism. It has been estimated that between a quarter and a half of alcoholics have had an alcoholic parent or close relative and that the children of alcoholic parents are twice as likely to become alcoholics as the children of non-alcoholic parents. This figure is the more alarming when it is considered that in America, for example, there are more than 28 million children of alcoholic parents. While this family tendency was once believed to result exclusively from the environmental situation, there is now evidence that there is an hereditary component.

Families with an alcoholic member (usually the father) are subjected to violence, loss of family cohesion, a good deal of continuing tension, and difficulties in social interactions.

Alcohol and accidents

Alcohol intoxication can lead to the type of fearless and foolhardy behaviour which not only makes a party swing but also leads to tragic consequences, especially as a result of traffic, domestic and industrial accidents.[5]

After two double whiskies, experienced bus drivers have been known to attempt to drive through a gap 14 inches narrower than their vehicles. Impairment of performance is detectable in drivers at levels as low as 30mg/100ml, and at a level of 80mg/100ml (the legal limit in Britain). The mean deterioration in performance is about 12 per cent. At this level, drivers are significantly more likely to be involved in accidents. The risk is about ten times higher than normal at 150mg/100ml and 20 times higher at 200mg/100ml.

The World Health Organisation estimates than in Australia, for example, at least 50 per cent of the deaths resulting from traffic accidents are associated with alcohol consumption. This type of alcohol-related accidents kills more people than all the infectious diseases put together. The percentage of traffic accidents which can be *attributed* to alcohol varies from country to country and appears to be as low as three to ten per cent in some; but even these low figures should exert some influence upon social policy and our attitude towards the drunken driver.

The table below shows that in Great Britain setting a legal limit of 80mg/100ml had a clear effect on the number of thousands of fatal or serious road accidents between 10 pm and 4 am.

Blood alcohol levels

BALs are usually quoted as milligrams of alcohol per 100 millilitres of blood or as a percentage. In 1954, the WHO Expert Committee on Alcohol reported that the inference cannot be avoided that at a blood alcohol concentration of about 50mg per 100ml (0·05 per cent), a statistically significant impairment of performance is observed.

The legal limit for driving is 80mg per 100ml in England, France and a few other European countries, 50mg in Sweden and 100mg in some of the states of the United States. A level of 80mg or 0·08 per cent can be expected if a man of average weight rapidly consumes two pints of beer or two double whiskies.

Alcohol is also implicated in a significant proportion of domestic and industrial accidents. One study of accidents at work in a Paris region found that ten to 15 per cent were probably due to alcohol intoxication. Another study of non-traffic accident victims in Switzerland between 1964 and 1970 showed that 24 per cent of them were under the influence of alcohol when they were brought into hospital. It is clear that alcohol adds considerably to the risks of any occupation in which accidents are avoided only by vigilance and clear heads.

Society's response

For thousands of years, in nearly every culture and historical period, men, women and even children have heeded Omar Khayyam's advice: 'While you live, drink!—for, once dead, you never shall return.'

In moderation, alcohol is a pleasure. However, there is now no doubt that alcohol can damage if taken in excess. Livers have been shot to pieces and families ruined; children have been harmed by their drinking parents and alcoholics have destroyed their own self-esteem. Because alcohol is addictive and because heavy drinking leads on to psychological, social and physical harm we must be concerned by the recent increase in alcoholic consumption throughout the world.

At the very least, governments, social scientists and the helping professions should be committed to a policy of preventing national *per capita* alcohol consumption from rising above their present levels. Self-help, social, psychological and medicinal interventions must be clearly described and evaluated. Finally, we must get away from the restrictive 'disease' model of alcoholism[6] and ask in what ways common drinking problems can be prevented, and in what ways the heavy drinker can be helped to modify his own drinking habits.

10 The search for cures

Recent pharmacological discoveries mean that the typical alcoholic or drug addict who is admitted to a hospital or detoxification unit will probably not experience very severe withdrawal symptoms. Within a couple of weeks his nervous system will be almost back to normal. Similarly, most smokers are able to abstain for a couple of weeks even though they may feel below par. For those who experience severe withdrawal, there is now nicotine chewing gum. It is relatively easy to help the addict to stop for a short time—long enough to overcome withdrawal symptoms. But what happens to the addicted person during the year following treatment? Once he has 'kicked the habit' or 'taken the cure' how easy is it to remain abstinent and adjust to a life without drugs?

We need to state again that it is often only the more severely dependent person who goes to a doctor or clinic for formal treatment. The picture that emerges when we look at the results of formal treatment may not apply to those who give up on their own.

If we use total abstinence as the sole criterion for success, we get the rather gloomy picture seen in Figure 1. Most studies show that people who ask for help will tend to improve in terms of the intensity of drug use (for example, in the number of days drunk) and in terms of social adjustment (such as the number of days worked) during the months which follow treatment. However, even very intensive and expensive forms of treatment do not appear to ensure this improvement. If we make adjustments for the characteristics of people who enter different treatment programmes, the improvement is as likely to occur with brief and simple treatment as it is with more elaborate and expensive approaches.[1]

Treatments for dependence

Traditionally, 'treatments' for drug dependence are discussed drug by drug. Opiate dependence is considered apart from the treatment of alcoholism which, in turn, is considered apart from tobacco dependence. Certainly in terms of biological effects,

She's grown used to the support of alcohol —will she be able to adjust to life without this prop?

withdrawal syndromes and social attitudes about the behaviours, there are substantial distinctions; but there are also strong similarities among treatments that help us see that all of the addictive disorders have certain common features.

There are a number of ways to classify treatments for drug dependence. One way is to divide them into two major categories. First, there are those which attempt to separate the individual from the specific drug of dependence as quickly as possible and then help him stay abstinent. The second approach is usually reserved for those who have unsuccessfully tried to stop. This provides either a substitute drug or a different way of using the original drug so that the harmful consequences of drug use are minimised. The use of substitute drugs often represents a temporary pause in the struggle, and the individual is eventually expected to try to give up the drug completely.

Within each of the two broad categories there are many subcategories and specific treatment programmes that vary with the theoretical orientation of the therapist and the specific drug of dependence. Brief surveys of the treatment of opioid dependence, cigarette smoking and alcoholism may provide some idea of the many possible variations.

Help for the opioid user

A century ago, the treatment of opioid dependence focused on two issues: easing the discomfort of the withdrawal syndrome, and re-educating 'the will'. Experts argued about the advantages of gradual reduction of dosage (over a period of weeks or months) as against abrupt reduction (immediate discontinuation or reduction of dose over a few days). This controversy is alive, and physicians are still trying to find non-opioid substances to ease the withdrawal syndrome—just as they have been for more than 100 years. The term 're-education of the will' has been replaced by 'treating the underlying factors that lead to drug use'.

Today, there are a number of accepted techniques for helping the opioid user get over the worst of the withdrawal syndrome. If the level of physical dependence is low, as it tends to be when young people are using illicit heroin, it is sometimes enough to provide emotional support and a place where the drug is unavailable. A number of therapeutic communities have made a ritual of having the heroin user kick 'cold turkey' on the living room couch.

When the degree of physical dependence is higher, the intensity of withdrawal can be reduced by giving small doses of any opioid drug, since they all act at the same receptors in the nervous system. Oral methadone is a popular drug for alleviating withdrawal because of its long duration of action. Withdrawal can be handled in a hospital, in a therapeutic community or at home: much depends on resolve and the level of motivation of the patient.

Properly managed, the most distressing part of withdrawal syndrome from shorter-acting opioids such as heroin and morphine is largely over after five to six days. With opioids such as methadone that stay in the body a long time, moderate withdrawal symptoms may persist for several weeks. In either case, relapse to opioids after completion of withdrawal has been, and remains, a major problem.

In the United States, among urban heroin addicts who came into formal treatment programmes, 70–90 per cent relapse within twelve months. This discouraging statistic has stimulated two very different therapeutic responses: one is to look for ways to correct the factors believed to lead to relapse; the second is to provide some addicts with opioids through legitimate channels.

Preventing relapse

For a number of years it was argued that opioids were used to control feelings that had their origins in childhood. The medical profession has therefore tried to use psychotherapeutic techniques that were developed for the treatment of neurosis. To date, not a single controlled study indicates that psychotherapy helps in preventing relapse. Prolonged (four to 18 months) hospitalisation (with or without psychotherapy), whether or not psychotherapy followed discharge, appeared to have no impact on relapse rate.

The support of other ex-addicts is one of the strongest motivations for kicking the habit.

In the United States, withdrawal (detoxification) sometimes followed by long-term psychotherapy and long periods of hospitalisation were the major approaches. Then in 1958, Chuck Dederich, a former alcoholic, established Synanon, a self-regulating community of former heroin addicts. In Synanon's

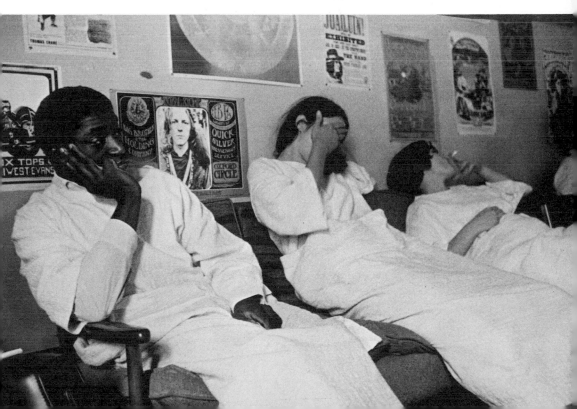

The loss of the drug support can be compensated for by finding the support of friendships.

view, the heroin addict was an immature 'emotional infant' who demanded instant gratification. The treatment consisted not of exploring the past and the parent's responsibility for the addict's present feelings, but of confronting the addict with his attempts to evade responsibility for his own behaviour. This was done in small groups run by other former addicts.

The addict was given appropriate rewards for responsible behaviour within the community. The rewards included affection and the esteem of his peers; but he would also be humiliated verbally and punished with loss of status for deviant behaviour. When he was first admitted, the addict was given menial tasks, but could rise rapidly in status over a period of months. The hierarchical structure of the community and the use of status and privilege were real-life application of the principles of behavioural modification. The ultimate punishment was to be expelled from the community.

Growth of communities

Within a few years, other self-regulating communities were set up in other parts of the United States. Many of them were started by former addicts who had some experience at Synanon.

While Synanon was pointedly anti-professional, deriding the relevance of psychological or psychiatric skills, other communities (Daytop Village, Phoenix House, Odyssey House, Gateway) were an amalgam of ex-addicts and more traditional professional leadership. In most of these communities, the treatment is required to last the 12–18 months of residence; but very few addicts who enter remain that long.

Follow-up studies show that a substantial percentage of heroin addicts who do manage to stay the course for more than a few months show remarkable decreases in drug use and criminal behaviour for several years after they leave: the longer they stay the better they do.[2] However, controlled studies are lacking.

Unfortunately the rigorous demands of therapeutic communities, and the expectation of a 12- to 18-month residence, limits the appeal of this approach to most addicts. At present, a considerable proportion of those who volunteer for treatment do so only when it is the alternative to an equal time in jail.

Outpatient counselling

In the United States, there are a number of programmes that offer individual or group 'counselling' to addicts who want to remain outpatients. Such counselling can occur before or after a period of detoxification, and is generally directed at real-life problems—employment, legal difficulties, and marital conflicts. Some programmes offer health services and vocational rehabilitation services. While this appears to be a humanitarian response, there is little evidence that such outpatient counselling alters the natural history of the disorder. Follow-up studies show that some addicts appear to be doing better a year or two later; but so are many who stopped treatment after a single visit.

There are even a few treatment programmes that have tried to deal with 'conditioned withdrawal symptoms'. These programmes, in addition to the usual counselling, have offered addicts an opportunity to take long-acting opioid antagonists such as naltrexone or cyclazocine. These drugs occupy the opioid receptors, but produce little or no action of their own. In this way, they prevent opioid drugs like heroin from producing their usual effects.

Theoretically if an addict taking an antagonist experiences a 'craving' for heroin (due to conditioned withdrawal or any other reason) and gives in to the use of heroin, he will experience no relief of withdrawal and no narcotics 'high'. Even if the heroin is used repeatedly, physical dependence will not develop because the heroin does not get to the receptor. Eventually the capacity of environmental stimuli to elicit conditioned withdrawal should fade out or 'extinguish', and the highly reinforced pattern of injecting drugs should weaken because the injection is not followed by the reinforcing of the drug. Unfortunately, addicts are not eager to take antagonists over long periods and researchers cannot yet show that this approach makes any long-term difference.[3]

There are many other approaches designed to increase the addict's motivation to tolerate withdrawal, or to decrease the internal tension believed to contribute to the desire to use opioids after withdrawal is over. These include hypnosis, acupuncture, Transcendental Meditation and biofeedback. Despite any theoretical value these approaches may have, there are as yet no scientifically controlled studies which have shown them to be of significant long-term value, a situation remarkably similar to that seen with alcoholism.

Opioid substitutes
Programmes providing natural opiates or using synthetic opioids such as methadone represent the second major category of approaches to opioid dependence. These programmes generally provide treatment only to individuals who have been unsuccessful at achieving abstinence in other ways.

The philosophy underlying the treatment varies. Dole and Nyswander, who first used methadone as a treatment, believed the drug was correcting a metabolic abnormality that was caused by the prolonged use of opioids. Such an abnormality produced a sense of 'drug hunger' each time the individual tried to give up the use of opioids. Originally high doses of methadone (100mg) were used which, in addition to suppressing 'drug hunger', produced a cross-tolerance to other opioids. For practical purposes, the individual on methadone got little or no reinforcing effects if he or she injected heroin. Dole and Nyswander referred to this as 'blockade'.

Although it is obvious that the patients treated by 'heroin blockade' are still physically dependent on large doses of an opioid, the behavioural, psychological, economic and medical consequences of this type of dependence are very different from those of using illicit heroin by the intravenous route. Methadone is long-acting drug. When it is taken by mouth there is a sharp onset of effects and they wear off very slowly, so that it is taken only once a day. Because there are no sharp ups and downs, the behaviour of the user is for practical purposes normal. Even a trained observer would be unable to pick out a person maintained on methadone.

Some clinicians take the view that opioid dependent people may be treating themselves for a variety of 'bad feelings', such as depression or low self-esteem, and that until we can find ways to treat these feelings we should provide the opioids at low cost to those who seem unable or unwilling to give them up. Clinicians also differ on when and how finally to withdraw drugs like methadone. While many people who were once maintained on methadone now totally abstain from all opioids, there are others who have great difficulty no matter how gradually the dose of the drug is reduced.

There is speculation that several different subgroups exist among those who seek treatment. One group may have some abnormality of the brain's own opioid transmitter system, and it is sometimes argued that the use of external drugs is a way to correct this abnormality. At present there is no evidence for this view. It is known that a significant proportion of opioid users experience depressed mood (suicide is not rare among this group, just as it is all too frequent among alcoholics) but the relationship between depression and relapse is still not clear.

Time to stop smoking

'Maybe I'll just have one... just this once...'

'Giving up smoking is easy. I've done it thousands of times.' With these words, Mark Twain put his finger on the major problem in the treatment of cigarette dependence as well as all other addictions—the problem of relapse. Once a smoker decides that it is time to stop, it is relatively easy to help him or her to give up smoking for a few weeks. But it is considerably more difficult to prevent the behaviour from starting up again in the following months or years.

Many smokers can stop on their own if they develop sufficient resolve. Yet there are many who have tried to go it alone and have been unsuccessful. The alternatives for them can be divided into two main categories—self-help procedures and organised treatment programmes.

Self-help procedures include books, kits, records and cigarettes that offer the smoker techniques for analysing his or her habit and then for systematically eliminating it. Also included are various filters and devices that are supposed to help the smoker gradually to wean himself from cigarettes. So far there have been no long-term evaluations of these self-help approaches.

Treatment programmes

Jerome Schwartz, who has reviewed the long-term results of a wide array of treatments for smoking, classified organised programmes into ten major categories: individual counselling, educational programmes, groups, medication, hypnosis, aversive conditioning, self-control, mass media, community approaches and miscellaneous.[4]

Individual counselling can range from counselling by physicians or nurses to individual psychotherapy. The latter is rarely employed but there is some evidence that the former actually has some short-term impact.

One very popular educational type of withdrawal programme is the '5-Day Plan', consisting mostly of lectures to relatively large groups.

Meetings take place on five consecutive days. Participants are shown smoke-damaged lungs and given a regimen of hot and cold showers, physical exercise, balanced diet and the avoidance of coffee, tea, cola drinks and alcohol. A substantial proportion of participants do stop smoking for a time; but the relapse rate is exceedingly high. Less than 25 per cent of those initially successful are still non-smokers twelve months later.

A number of group programmes have been developed. They may be operated by profit-making organisations or non-profit groups such as the American Cancer Society. The groups generally represent an amalgam of group processes (learning theory, inspiration and exhortation). They are usually conducted by former smokers and consist of one session a week for eight to ten weeks. They often provide a well-planned series of preparatory steps, together with group support and helpful hints for dealing with withdrawal and situations likely to be associated with relapse.

The use of medication to alleviate withdrawal or to create an aversion to the taste of cigarettes has not yet proved to be of any significant value, although the recent development of nicotine chewing gum shows some promise.

Making smoking aversive
More recently, there has been considerable interest in a treatment strategy that tries to make smoking itself aversive in order to counteract any pleasure derived from cigarettes. The most popular techniques involve either rapid smoking at the rate of one puff every six seconds, or smoking while warm smoky air is blown into the face. Both procedures cause some discomfort and even nausea.

Doctor Edward Lichtenstein and his colleagues working at the University of Oregon have carried out the bulk of the research on these techniques. In one study it was discovered that rapid smoking, warm smoky air and a combination of both were all

117

Simple to hide it from the world— but not so easy to hide from the consequences.

equally effective and resulted in quite a high rate of abstinence six months after treatment (60 per cent). A control group who were given the same amount of attention, but no aversive therapy, and a drug designed to help them control their smoking achieved only 30 per cent abstinence at the six month follow-up assessment.

These results suggest that associating smoking with an unpleasant experience results in a conditioned aversion to cigarettes. However, another experiment carried out by Harris and Lichtenstein suggested a different conclusion. This experiment aimed to assess the importance of the way in which the therapist interacts with the client. Although all clients received 'rapid smoking' treatment, only half of them received strong encouragement and praise. This group of clients were addressed by their first names, the therapist told them of his own success in using rapid smoking to kick the habit and enthusiastically communicated a strong expectation of success.

During treatment, clients were praised for all successes and at all time the therapist's aim was to motivate, encourage and reward. The other groups were told simply that they were taking part in an experiment to test the effectiveness of 'rapid smoking' and all interactions between client and therapist were rather brief and impersonal.

Three months after treatment, there were marked differences between the two groups, convincingly demonstrating that *what the therapist says* is of paramount importance; 72 per cent of the group who received strong encouragement were abstinent after three months, compared with only six per cent of the group who were given no expectation of success and only a low level of praise and encouragement.

The most sensible conclusion that we can draw from current scientific literature is that this form of treatment is, by itself, of little or no value, but that the social context in which the treatment is given is crucially important and should be the focus of future research.

Other approaches

Another fashionable approach with wide popular appeal involves hypnosis. However, in 1971, Johnstone and Donoghue reviewed relevant studies and concluded that 'although there are many clinical reports available, there is almost no good research evidence attesting to the effectiveness of hypnosis in the elimination of smoking behaviour'. Their conclusion is still valid today.

Many other treatments have been tried, including electrical aversion, acupuncture, yoga, biofeedback, relaxation training, desensitisation and sensory deprivation. These studies nearly always show that whatever the treatment approach, good results tend to be achieved at the end of treatment but very poor results are reported when clients are re-assessed one year later. This suggests that further research should concentrate on devising methods of preventing relapse.[5]

In the absence of a generally accepted, proven technique that works for everyone, the smoker who wants to become an ex-smoker should become his own scientist. It is probable that different approaches work for different people and the best advice that can be given to a smoker is to experiment with different methods until he or she find one that works. If there is a group or help available from a warm, sympathetic therapist, then so much the better. Above all relapse should not lead to pessimism. Long-term success is often preceded by a temporary failure. In terms of reducing risks to health, the effort is a good investment.

Helping the alcoholic

Many medical practitioners offer very little help to the alcoholic because they believe that it is difficult, or even impossible, to produce any permanent change from a brief interview. They tend to refer alcoholic patients to the nearest special treatment programme.

At these programmes, psychiatrists, psychologists and social workers are usually involved in giving drugs, advice and support and most have facilities for admitting the alcoholic to a hospital if necessary. In hospital, total abstinence from alcohol is nearly always the rule and treatment will involve drug therapy for withdrawal symptoms and depression, group therapy which attempts to make sure that the alcoholic is facing up to his problem (usually called his disease), and continuing psycho-therapy from a psychiatrist or psychologist.

Participation in Alcoholics Anonymous groups during this period is encouraged or may even be a required part of treatment. The treatment usually lasts between four weeks and three months with continued outpatient help during the period immediately after discharge. Only recently has the effectiveness of this approach been tested.

Dr Griffith Edwards, Dr Jim Orford and their colleagues working at the Maudsley Hospital in London decided to compare this intensive treatment approach with another approach involving just one brief contact, during which some advice and encouragement was given, followed by visits from a social worker. A hundred alcoholic men were randomly assigned to the 'advice' or 'intensive treatment' conditions. Fifty had just a very brief contact with the hospital, while the rest had the more usual form of psychiatric treatment, including encouragement to take a medicine (similar to Antabuse) that causes an unpleasant reaction if the patient drinks alcohol.

For two years after treatment, alcohol consumption as well as vocational, marital and social problems were recorded. It was found that there were no differences at all between the two groups: both did reasonably well, with about half still showing improved social adjustment at two years. This is not an isolated result since there are now a number of other studies showing that a long period of hospital treatment (three weeks to three months) is no more effective than a brief period (three weeks or less) and that, as in studies of opioid and cigarette dependence, many specific treatment interventions have not been shown to be more effective in the long term than what might have been expected as a result of the natural course of events.

Learning to hate alcohol

Aversion therapy has probably been one of the most widely used techniques and the aim of this form of treatment does not seem to be unreasonable. A treatment which replaces a craving for alcohol with a feeling of revulsion, if at all possible, would be welcomed by many alcoholics the world over.

There are two main forms of aversion therapy: electrical and chemical. In the former, moderate electric shock is applied either by the therapist or by the patient himself as he deliberately thinks about or actually consumes his favourite alcoholic beverage. Chemical aversion involves the consumption of a drug which causes the alcoholic to feel nauseous or actually vomit as he smells, tastes and swallows alcohol.

There are now very strong reasons for believing that electrical aversion is ineffective but no evidence to allow us to make a decision about chemical aversion, since there is no well-designed trial which provides the information on which to base a decision. The proliferation of aversion techniques without adequate testing is one of the scandals of our times. Although there are more than 400 reports in scientific literature, most of the investigations of chemical aversion are of such poor quality that we are still unable to decide whether or not these unpleasant techniques are of any special help at all to the alcoholic.

Not all gloom

The scientific literature on the treatment of alcoholism forces us to be realistic but not pessimistic. We now know that intensive treatment does not always lead to better results than simpler and briefer forms of treatment. The alcoholic and his family should not expect miracle cures, but the likelihood that things will improve is reasonably good.[1,6,7] What is uncertain is the degree to which formal treatment contributes to the other environmental factors that are part of the natural healing process.

Many alcoholics have achieved long-term sobriety through Alcoholics Anonymous. The alcoholic and the helping professions must learn from them and make full use of their experience and commitment. A.A. was the brain-child of a stockbroker, Bill W., and a medical practitioner, Dr Bob. The first was formed in Ohio in 1935. It is now a world-wide organisation claiming well over one million active members. The self-help process of A.A. involves not only mutual support, identification and shared experiences, but also 'coping through involvement', so that sobriety is achieved by becoming actively involved, attending meetings, helping others, office holding, attending A.A. events and much more besides.

Other forms of treatment have been developed and systematically tested. Many of these, such as self-control training, social skills training, assertive training and relaxation training, attempt to teach the alcoholic how to cope with his own personal problems. For example, Nathan Azrin, working at the Anna State Hospital in the United States, has had encouraging results by helping the alcoholic to deal with social, vocational and marital problems. Azrin's approach, which he calls 'community reinforcement', aims to help the alcoholic develop strong bonds with his community by practising and developing the skills needed in all kinds of social interactions, whether it be conversing, relating to one's spouse, or being interviewed for a job.

Alcohol in moderation

Several follow-up studies have found that there can be markedly improved social functioning within total abstinence. Some researchers have now begun to ask whether certain alcoholics can be taught to drink in moderation.

Mark and Linda Sobell, of Vanderbilt University in Tennessee, have reported some success in helping a small group of moderately dependent alcoholics to drink without drinking to excess. Treatments were individually tailored to each client's needs, but usually involved a videotaped replay of the patient's drunken behaviour in order to increase motivation for treatment; analysis of the situations and experiences associated with excessive drinking; the planning of alternative methods of coping, and practice at controlled drinking in a simulated bar and in a simulated home environment. Evidently, 'controlled drinking' is an appropriate goal for some—but only some—alcoholics.[7]

Common factors in drug abuse

One of the most hopeful trends in the 'peculiar business of helping people to change their behaviour' is the emergence of a set of concepts with general applicability to more than one drug. It is becoming clear, for example, that price, availability and social attitude are very important factors which influence all drug use and abuse. Drug dependence of all types is also, to some extent, prevented or ameliorated by good social support so that one component of treatment is usually directed towards marital and social relationships.

The basic difficulty for the smoker, the alcoholic and the heroin addict is to avoid relapse, since coming off the drug for a few days or weeks is usually not a great problem. Relapse into tobacco, alcohol or heroin use is often precipitated by similar crises, such as experiences of failure, hopelessness, depression and anger. In addition, the very presence of the drug—whether tobacco, alcohol or heroin—can accentuate the experience of 'craving'. Furthermore, there is often a tendency to abuse more than one drug. For instance, heroin addicts and alcoholics nearly always smoke heavily as well.

The future of the drug dilemma

Freedom carries risks. People often choose short-term benefits over long-term gains. This is as true with respect to physical and mental wellbeing as it is in the realm of economics and politics. The use of any drug, whether to treat a disease state, a feeling of psychic discomfort, or to make us more relaxed and sociable, carries some degree of risk. This risk may be in terms of adverse physical effects, unwanted behavioural effects, or long-term adverse consequences. The latter can be in the sphere of the physical (e.g. lung cancer from smoking or cirrhosis from alcohol use) or in terms of altered relationships to life's other activities. In its extreme form, such altered relationship can lead to a life that is dominated if not destroyed by the use of a drug.

Some of the techniques used by society to limit use of drugs seem counterproductive. Torture and execution of tobacco users under Sultam Murad IV were undoubtedly a deterrent, but, except among the most enthusiastic opponents of smoking, such an approach would no longer be viewed as acceptable. As in the case of penny gin in 18th century England ('drunk for a penny; dead drunk for two'), and of cigarette smoking in most countries today, the adverse effects of drug use are due most often to the inability of the society to develop acceptable ways to structure and limit drug use.

We must therefore end as we began—with the recognition that the problems of drug use and abuse are difficult and demand both wisdom and a flexible response. Easy availability and low cost make it far more likely that a substance will be widely used, and wide use increases the proportion of problem use and the proportion of the population that exhibits dependence. Societies the world over are now looking for practical and acceptable ways to limit availability and raise costs in order to prevent the problems that drugs can cause. This is so whether the drugs are defined as legal recreational (tobacco and alcohol), where the techniques are taxes and licensing, or legal therapeutic (anti-anxiety drugs, pain killers or amphetamines), where the techniques involve restriction on medical prescribing, or entirely prohibited drugs (marijuana, LSD), where the restrictive techniques involve fines and criminal penalties for distribution or possession.

We continue to hope that people of all ages will learn to find greater satisfaction in living rather than in some elusive chemical nirvana, but it is unlikely that the problem of drug use and abuse will be 'solved' now or in the future. Each new generation must wrestle with the seductive rediscovery of substances whose initial use is so beguiling that they tempt the user to continue and to ignore the risks.

References

1 Introducing addiction

1. Brecher, E. M. *Licit and Illicit Drugs*. Boston: Little, Brown, 1972.
2. Levine, H. G. The discovery of addiction. *J. Stud Alcohol*, 39: 143–174, 1978.
3. World Health Organisation Expert Committee on Drug Dependence. Twentieth Report. Technical Report Series 551, WHO, Geneva, 1974.
4. Jaffe, J. H. "Drug addiction and drug abuse", in *The Pharmacological Basis of Therapeutics*, 5th ed., Eds L. S. Goodman and A. Gilman. New York: Macmillan, 1975.

2 Why are drugs abused?

1. Woods, J. H. "Behavioral Pharmacology of Drug Self-Administration", in *Psychopharmacology: A Generation of Progress*, M. A. Lipton, A. DiMascio and K. Killam. New York: Raven Press, 1978.
2. Mello, N. K. "Stimulus Self-Administration: Some Implications for the Prediction of Drug Abuse Liability", in *Predicting Dependence Liability of Stimulant and Depressant Drugs*, Eds T. Thompson and K. R. Unna. Baltimore: University Park Press, 1977.
3. Robins, L. N. "Addict Careers", in *Handbook on Drug Abuse*, Eds R. I. Du Pont, A. Goldstein and J. O'Donnell. Washington, D. C.: U.S. Government Printing Office, 1979.
4. Chein, I., Gerard, D. L., Lee, R. S. and Rosenfield, E. *The Road to H: Narcotics, Delinquency and Social Policy*. New York: Basic Books, 1964.
5. Goodwin, D. W. Alcoholism and Heredity. *Archives of General Psychiatry*, 36: 57–64, 1979.
6. Jaffe, J. H. "Drug Addiction and Drugs Abuse", in *The Pharmacological Basis of Therapeutics*, 5th ed., Eds L. S. Goodman and A. Gilman. New York: Macmillan, 1975.
7. Mello, N. K. and Mendelson, J. H. "Clinical Aspects of Alcohol Dependence", in *Drug Addiction I. Vol. 45, I, Handbook of Experimental Pharmacology*, Ed. Wm R. Martin. Berlin: Springer-Verlag, 1977.
8. Mirin, S. M., Meyer, R. E., and McNamee, H. B. Psychopathology, craving, and mood during heroin acquisition: An experimental study. *International Journal of Addictions*, 11: 525–544, 1976.
9. O'Brien, C. P., Testa, T., O'Brien, T. J., Brady, J. P. and Wells. Conditioned narcotic withdrawal in humans. *Science* 195: 1000–1002, 1977.

3 Pursuing the poppy

1. Brecher, E. M. *Licit and Illicit Drugs*. Boston: Little, Brown, 1972.
2. Snyder, S. H. Opiate receptors and internal opiates. *Scientific American* 236: 44–67, 1977.
3. Jaffe, J. H. "Drug addiction and drug abuse", in *The Pharmacological Basis of Therapeutics*, 5th ed., Eds L. S. Goodman and A. Gilman. New York: Macmillan 1975.
4. Stimson, G. V. *Heroin and Behavior*, New York: John Wiley, 1973.
5. Stimson, G. V., Oppenheimer, E., and Thorley, A. Seven-year follow-up of heroin addicts: Drug use and outcome. *British Med. J.*, 1: 1190–1192, 1978.
6. Robins, L. N. "Addict Careers", in *Handbook on Drug Abuse*, Eds R. I. Du Pont, A. Goldstein, and J. O'Donnell. Washington, D.C.: U.S. Government Printing Office, 1979.

4 Looking for a lift

1. Brecher, E. M. *Licit and Illicit Drugs*. Boston: Little, Brown, 1972.
2. Kalant, O. J. *The Amphetamines: Toxicity and Addiction*. Springfield, Illinois: C. C. Thomas, 1966.
3. Ellinwood, E. J., Jr. "Amphetamine and cocaine", in *Psychopharmacology in the Practice of Medicine*, Ed. M. E. Jarvik. New York: Appleton-Century-Crofts, 1977.
4. Grinspoon, L. and Bakalar, J. B. *Cocaine—A Drug and Its Social Evolution*. New York: Basic Books, 1976.
5. Petersen, R. C. and Stillman, R. C. *Cocaine: 1977*. Washington, D.C.: U.S. Government Printing Office, 1977.

5 Down with anxiety

1. Wesson, D. R. and Smith, D. E., *Barbiturates: Their use, Misuse and Abuse*. New York: Human Sciences Press, 1977.
2. Jaffe, J. H. "Drug addiction and drug abuse", *The Pharmacological Basis of Therapeutics*, 5th ed., Eds L. S. Goodman and A. Gilman. New York: Macmillan, 1975.
3. Brecher, E. M. *Licit and Illicit Drugs*, Boston: Little, Brown, 1972.
4. *Review of Inhalants: Euphoria to Dysfunction*. N.I.D.A. Research Monograph 15, Eds C. W. Sharp and M. L. Brehm. U.S. Dept of Health Education and Welfare, U.S. Superintendent of Documents. Washington, D.C.: U.S. Government Printing Office, 1977.
5. Cohen, S. "Inhalants", in *Handbook on Drug Abuse*, Eds R. I. Du Pont, A. Goldstein, and J. O'Donnell. Washington D.C.: U.S. Government Printing Office, 1979.

6 The chemistry of mysticism

1. Cohen, S. *The Beyond Within*. New York: Athenium, 1964.
2. Brecher, E. M. *Licit and Illicit Drugs*, Boston: Little, Brown, 1972.
3. Hollister, L. E. *Chemical Psychoses: LSD and Related Drugs*. Springfield, Illinois: C. C. Thomas, 1972.
4. *PCP—Phencyclidine Abuse: An Appraisal*. In: N.I.D.A. Research Monograph 21, Eds R. C. Petersen and R. C. Stillman. Washington, D.C.: U.S. Government Printing Office, 1978.

7 Marijuana—drug for all seasons

1. ——, *Marijuana and Health*, Seventh Annual Report to the U.S. Congress from the Secretary of Health, Education and Welfare. Washington, D.C.: U.S. Government Printing Office, 1979.
2. Jones, R. "Human effects (of marijuana)", in Marijuana, Research Findings: 1976. N.I.D.A. Research Monograph 14, Ed. R. C. Petersen. Washington, D.C.: U.S. Government Printing Office, 1977.
3. Rubin, V. and Comitas, L. *Ganja in Jamaica: The effects of Marijuana*. New York: Anchor/ Doubleday, 1976.
4. *Pharmacology of Marijuana*. Eds M. C. Braude and S. Szara. New York: Raven Press, 1976.
5. *Hashish—Studies of Long-term Use*. Eds C. Stefanis, R. Dornbush and M. Fink. New York: Raven Press, 1977.

8 Tobacco—the devil's weed

1. Corti, E. *A History of Smoking*. New York: Harcourt Brace Jovanovich, 1932.
2. "Smoking and Health", in *DHEW Publication Number (PHS) 79–50066*, Eds Office on Smoking and Health. Washington, D.C.: U.S. Government Printing Office, 1979, various chapters.

3. Russell, M. A. H. and Feyerabend, C. Cigarette smoking: A dependence on high-nicotine boli. *Drug Metab. Rev.*, 8: 29–57, 1978.
4. Jaffe, J. H., and Jarvik, M. D. "Tobacco use and tobacco use disorder", in *Psychopharmacology: A Generation of Progress*, Eds M. A. Lipton, A. Di Mascio, and K. F. Killam. New York: Raven Press, 1978.
5. Hutchinson, R. R. and Emley, G. S. "Effects of nicotine on avoidance, conditioned suppression and aggression response measures in animals and man", in *Smoking Behavior: Motives and Incentives*, Ed. W. L. Dunn, Jr. Washington, D.C.: Winston, 1973.

9 Alcohol and alcoholism

1. Miller, P. M. *Behavioural Treatment of Alcoholism*. Oxford: Pergamon, 1976.
2. Calahan, D. and Cisin, I. H. Epidemiological and social factors associated with drinking problems. In R. E. Tarter and A. A. Sugerman (Eds.). *Alcoholism.* Massachusetts, Addison-Wesley, 1976.
3. World Health Organization. *Alcohol-Related Disabilities.* (Offset Publication No. 32). Geneva: WHO, 1977.
4. British Royal College of Psychiatrists Report. *Alcohol and Alcoholism.* London. Tavistock Publications, 1979.
5. Moser, J. *Problems and Programmes Related to Alcohol and Drug Dependence in 33 Countries.* (Offset Publication No. 6). Geneva: WHO, 1974.
6. Pattison, E. M., Sobell, M. B. and Sobell, L. C. *Emerging Concepts of Alcohol Dependence.* New York: Springer, 1977.

10 The search for cures

1. Orford, J. and Edwards, G. *Alcoholism.* Institute of Psychiatry, Maudsley Monographs 26, Oxford University Press, 1977.
2. Simpson, D. D., Savage, J., and Lloyd, M. R. Follow-up evaluation of treatment of drug abuse during 1969 to 1972. *Archives General Psychiatry*, 36: 772–780, 1979.
3. Resnick, R. B., Schuyten-Resnick, E. and Washton, A. M. Narcotic antagonists in the treatment of opioid dependence: Review and commentary. *Comp. Psych.* Vol. 20, 2: 116–125, 1979.
4. Weissman, M. W., Slobetz, F., Prusoff, B., Mesritz, M. and Howard, P. Clinical depression among narcotic addicts maintained on methadone in the community. *Amer. J. of Psych.* 133: 1434–1438, 1976.
5. Schwartz, J. L. "Smoking Cures: Ways to Kick an Unhealthy Habit", in *Research on Smoking Behavior*, N.I.D.A. Research Monograph 17, Eds M. E. Jarvik, J. W. Cullen, E. R. Gritz, T. M. Vogt, and L. J. West. Washington, D.C.: U.S. Government Printing Office, 1977.
6. *Alcohol and Alcoholism.* The Report of a Special Committee of the Royal College of Psychiatrists. London: Tavistock Publications, 1979.
7. *The Diagnosis and Treatment of Alcoholism*, Eds J. H. Mendelson and N. K. Mello. New York: McGraw-Hill, 1979.

Index

Photo credits

Bandphoto—61; Barnaby's Picture Library—6 (*top*), 93, 105; Ron Chapman—100, 104; Gadi Dagon—34; John Garrett—59, 85; Henry Grant—31, 75; The Health Education Council—116; Kristal—90; Judy & Kenny Lester—111; Lisa Mackeson—38; Margaret Murray—102; Popperfoto—19, 40, 47, 86; Project Icarus—27; Rex—6 (*bottom*), 8, 13, 14 (*3*), 16 (*2*), 29, 35, 46, 50 (*2*), 55, 57, 63, 64, 76, 77, 79, 83, 84, 91, 96, 113, 114, 118, (Astral Photo) 9, (Edwin Karmiol) 52, (G. Sipahioglu) 18, 89, (Sipa Press) 5, 21, 22, 26, 39, 81, 88; Chris Schwarz—99; Chris Steele-Perkins—58, 82; Homer Sykes—24, 67, 70, 71, 92, 107; John Topham Picture Library—33; Vizo Paris—43.

Multimedia Publications Inc have endeavoured to observe the legal requirements with regard to the rights of the suppliers of graphic and photographic materials.